DONNE'S IMAGERY

A STUDY IN CREATIVE SOURCES

by

MILTON ALLAN RUGOFF

NEW YORK

RUSSELL & RUSSELL · INC

1962

ACKNOWLEDGMENT

I am glad of this opportunity to acknowledge my indebtedness to the various editors of Donne's works: to Mr. John Sparrow for his edition of the *Devotions*, to Mr. John Hayward for his editing of miscellaneous prose pieces, and, most of all, to Professor Herbert J. C. Grierson for his invaluable preparation and annotation of the poems. Of the doubtful pieces appended to Professor Grierson's edition it should be noted that I have used only the verse letter to Lady Huntingdon, "*That unripe side of earth*," which Professor Grierson himself admitted into the canon in his later one-volume edition.

Although I began my work on Donne's imagery before the appearance of Professor Caroline F. E. Spurgeon's *Shakespeare's Imagery*, I owe much to her analyses of the nature of imagery and her spirited and illuminating explorations of its potentialities.

For their suggestions and helpful criticisms of my work I wish to thank Professor Oscar J. Campbell, Professor William Y. Tindall, and Dr. Henry W. Wells of Columbia University. I profited, too, from the friendly advice of Professor Mark Van Doren, and thereby added to an old debt.

Most particularly I wish to express my gratitude to Professor Frank Allen Patterson of Columbia University for the guidance and encouragement he gave me from the beginning of this work to the end.

MILTON A. RUGOFF

. . . . our creatures are our thoughts, creatures that are borne Gyants; that reach from East to West, from Earth to Heaven, that doe not onely bestride all the Sea, and Land, but span the Sunn and Firmament at once; My thoughts reach all, comprehend all. Inexplicable mistery; I their Creator am in a close prison, in a sicke bed, any where, and any one of my Creatures, my thoughts, is with the Sunne, and beyond the Sunne, overtakes the Sunne, and overgoes the Sunne in one pace, one steppe, every where.

Donne in *Meditation IV*

CONTENTS

INTRODUCTION

INTRODUCTION

I

THE IMAGE AND ITS SIGNIFICANCE

Of the many ways in which the creative imagination of great writers has been approached, the most slighted, I think, is that of imagery. The explanation is, perhaps, not too far to seek, for no matter what other functions it may fulfill, the most conspicuous, if not the most significant function of imagery has always been that of embellishment. As such it has generally been treated by rhetoricians as one more technical adjunct of style, another of the hand-maidens of direct statement. Thus, under its rhetorical subdivisions of simile, metaphor, personification, allegory, and the like, it has been neatly tucked away in the strict pigeonholes of "figures of speech." When these have been disturbed or reconsidered it has most often been for the purpose of making new subdivisions or finer distinctions between them.

All this has a place and serves a purpose, but what it has almost completely obscured is the fact that an image is, in its content, one of the freest of the imaginative con-tributions that a writer may make to a given statement of meaning. Although the meaning he is trying to convey may govern the aim and purpose of the image, it will have no control over its substance and source; these the writer fixes upon almost at will. Because the image need meet the meaning of the passage only by way of analogy or illustration, the writer is left virtually untrammelled in his imaginative decision as to what its contents shall be. His fancy is given free rein—the wonderful liberty of de-veloping a parallel or analogy out of anything from heaven, earth or the infinite world of the mind. Given such free-

dom, he turns naturally and inevitably to those things
which, for reasons that lie as deep as personality itself, he
has found most interesting, most vivid, most memorable.
And in that exercise of choice, that almost arbitrary decision concerning what branch of learning or phase of life
he will draw his image from—when, of course, that choice
is repeated often enough or when it becomes part of a pattern—we get the most revelatory kind of glimpses into the
natural tides, drifts, and currents of a writer's creative
imagination.

When Donne, seeking to make clear the effect of a temporary parting on his relationship with his wife, writes:

> Our two soules therefore, which are one,
>   Though I must goe, endure not yet
> A breach, but an expansion,
>   Like gold to ayery thinnesse beate,

the image "like gold to ayery thinnesse beate" illuminates
the basic statement of meaning so perfectly that it sounds
almost inevitable. It subserves that meaning completely,
yet its substance or contents, the beating of gold to leaf,
constitutes a choice which is the free and peculiar contribution of Donne's imagination. One such choice may have
little significance, but when we find the writer drawing
again and again upon the same source, applying it sometimes to the same end but just as often to any variety of
ends, have we not struck upon one of the sources of his
imagination, upon a cache which is, for him, filled with
jewels not only fascinating in themselves but capable of
casting light on whatever is brought near them?

One of the most interesting things about the content
of images is that their disclosures are, in a sense, almost
unwitting. The writer, seeking an image which will contribute to his meaning, is more intent for the moment on

its analogousness, the effectiveness, that is, of the parallel, than on the source of its substance. For that substance he turns, as I have pointed out, to the things to which he is drawn naturally and almost unthinkingly by his particular tastes and peculiar temperament. Although he may polish and cherish each word of the image, he has little reason to pay conscious attention to the source from which he draws it—and no reason at all for noting the various classes of sources presented by the collected body of his images. The remarkable thing, then, is that although the image is a finished product of his art, the writer remains virtually unaware of what its contents, when studied along with thousands of others from his pen, may reveal.

It seems to me, moreover, equally important to point out not only that imagery is an essential part of that which is most purely imaginative in writing, but that the collected body of a writer's images is that essence isolated in as unified and comprehensive a form as such an essence can be isolated. Imagery is certainly not the only approach to the creative imagination, but I know of no other wherein the sheer bodyings forth of the creative fancy seem so open to isolation and definition, so plentiful, and so capable of presenting a convincingly rounded picture.

In this respect, possessing what has been referred to as "imaginative autonomy" *—an independence wherein its content is freely determined by the writer's fancy, imagery is very different from the mere references or allusions usually collected to secure an index to a writer's knowledge of botany, the Bible, law or the like. For the most part these are simply a part of the immediate subject matter, a courtroom scene in Shakespeare being inevitably accompanied by many allusions to the law, a sermon

---

* By J. M. Murry in his *Countries of the Mind,* Oxford University Press, 1931, p. 10.

by Donne just as inevitably accompanied by many allusions to theology, and so on. The study of such references may reveal much that is interesting and valuable but it makes no attempt to distinguish between the references essential to description or analysis—nine-tenths of which in Donne is theological—and those which represent the driftings and soarings of the unrestricted imagination. Where his obligation to a patron or his position as a priest in the Church of England may well have dictated the actual theme and substance respectively of a eulogistic poem and an Easter Day sermon, the figures of speech which he introduces into such pieces are virtually uncontrolled by extraneous considerations and embody pure imagination.

What I have said of the function of imagery applies, moreover, to every type of writing. Whether that writing be a collection of light lyrics or a volume of sermons, imagery can contribute its free-flowing imaginative undertone. And the flavor it imparts will become one of the characteristic distinctions of a writer. This is true of almost all writers; in the case of a few the imagery is so vivid or so definitely relied on for the illumination of meaning that it compels more than ordinary attention in any consideration of the nature or quality of their work. This has happened in the case of Donne—and more conspicuously, I dare say, than in any writer of the same rank. Through three centuries critic after critic has called attention—in some periods, to be sure, more for the purpose of blame than praise—to Donne's imagery. Whether for good or ill, the best known judgment ever passed on Donne and his "school", that of Samuel Johnson in his life of Cowley, characterized them almost exclusively in terms of their imagery; and virtually every general study of English literature has followed suit by giving prominent place to discussions of the so-called "metaphysical" image. Whether it be appropriate or not, the generic term "metaphysical poet", applied to Donne and those whom he is supposed to have influenced, has its roots in early attempts to characterize Donne's imagery. Yet, despite all that has been said about these images, no one has undertaken such an examination as might establish clearly and completely in what directions Donne really went in those strange excursions of fancy which have distinguished him in the eyes of critics and exercised so many of them.

With imagery presenting, as I have indicated, a large and extraordinarily varied group of authentic representatives of the creative imagination, the possibilities for exploration are virtually unlimited. We may observe tendencies on every level of the imagination, from the broadest, most basic proclivity to any one of the countless curious minor biases of fancy. And all along the way we may learn as much from what the writer avoids or slights as from that to which he turns and on which he concentrates. In the case of a writer like Donne we can seek to determine whether, for example, his imagination turned to books and learning, to everyday life, or to nature; or whether it was concerned with the scientific or the literary, the abstract or the concrete, the old or the new, the remote or the immediate, the fantastic or the real, the minute detail or the cosmic whole. Examining even more closely we can undertake from time to time to decide whether his fancy seemed more at home in open field or city street, in royal court or library, on the vast ocean or in the vaster grave; whether, finally, he drew more confidently on the lore of astronomer, courtier, conjurer, coiner or divine. Naturally, in determining such tendencies we may learn not only what the basic directions of his imagination are and what interests appear to lie closest to his heart but also what these contribute to the total impact of his writings. Thus, we may discover through the study of the sources of Donne's imagery not only that he has a compelling interest in, let us say, the sciences of his time but that the figures he draws from these are an essential part of that material whereby he transmutes passion into precise and objective terms and achieves that intellectual apprehension of emotion that is so vital a characteristic of his work.

Moreover, although such a mosaic of Donne's imagination pieced together from his imagery would be a self-sufficient, absolute statement of the nature of that imagery, the wealth of material supplied by Professor Caroline Spurgeon * concerning the imagery not only of Shakespeare but also of several other Elizabethans, including Marlowe and Bacon, offers opportunity after opportunity for comparison between Donne and his contemporaries, and enables us to place our conclusions on a relative basis at almost every point.

As is perhaps evident by now, the possible directions that may be taken in the study of the content and sources of imagery are almost bewildering in their variety and attractiveness. Each deposit of images is, moreover, so linked to the next that it is only by the constant exercise of restraint and the drawing of arbitrary lines that the student can keep in one main lode and out of the tempting cross-strains that face him at every turn. Thus, voluminous as her study of Shakespeare's imagery was, Professor Spurgeon pointed out again and again, by way of preface, that she had taken "merely a limited selection of literally dozens of directions" that might have been followed with profit—only pushing ajar one door, so to speak,

---

* In her *Shakespeare's Imagery and What It Tells Us,* New York, Macmillan, 1935; hereafter designated as *Spurgeon.*

to the fascinating and unexamined treasures that lay heaped beyond. So the first to venture out on the sea of Donne's imagery—although it be but a small body of water beside that of the great playwright and one rarely marked by similar vistas, variety or sheer beauty—must be content to chart only the main tides and perhaps a few of the more manifest of its strange currents and peculiar drifts.

II

THE NATURE OF THE EVIDENCE

In the preceding chapter I undertook to make clear the significance of imagery as a key to the creative imagination. It remains now to indicate by what methods it may be collected, classified, and made to yield its secrets. In these directions Professor Spurgeon has taken a number of important steps and her study of Shakespeare throws light at several points on the basic problems of the approach to creative sources through the content of imagery. We are dealing, however, with the pure stuff of imagination, with materials as peculiar to each writer as his personality; and we may expect each to present new problems and require vital adaptations in approach and procedure.

The first step, the actual collection of images, necessitates a moment's consideration of the scope of the term itself.* Since our main interest is in content and source, we may ignore almost completely the distinctions which have been set up among the various types of figures. Whether it be simile—

> And yet no greater, but more eminent,
> Love by the Spring is growne;
> As, in the firmament,
> Starres by the Sunne are not inlarg'd, but
> showne,

---

* Of the books that have been written on this question and on images in general, almost all seem to have approached the subject for the purpose of adding to or clarifying the distinctions between the various types of figures—a very interesting point of departure but not basically relevant to this study. See, for example, Henry W. Wells' *Poetic Imagery*, Columbia University Press, New York, 1924, and Stephen J. Brown's *The World of Imagery*, Kegan Paul, London, 1927.

metaphor—

> No Spring, nor Summer Beauty hath such grace,
> As I have seen in one Autumnall face,

personification—

> death is but a Groome,
> Which brings a Taper to the outward roome,

allegory, illustration, or those frequent figures wherein
several of these are inextricably combined, each serves our
purpose. All of these have in common the fact that they
introduce material by way of analogy or illustration to
clarify, embellish, heighten, or add to a given statement
of meaning; and if we need an explicit definition of an
image this may well serve. In any case it would be un-
necessary to go beyond Dr. Spurgeon's vivid summation:

> It is a description or an idea, which by compari-
> son or analogy, stated or understood, with some-
> thing else, transmits to us through the emotions or
> associations it arouses, something of its "whole-
> ness", the depth and richness of the way the writer
> views, conceives or has felt what he is telling us.*

These cover all the familiar figures of speech (except, it
should be noted, metonymy and synechdoche, which really
introduce no new images from without), and, in addition,
those images contributed by direct illustration. Nor, in
the sense in which we approach images, need we—or may
we—differentiate between the figures of prose and those of
poetry. There may, of course, be some difference in the
way the metaphor is presented or in the language in which
it is couched, but in the choice of its substance the imagination of the prose writer is, as we shall find, hardly less

* *Op. cit.,* p. 9.

free than that of the poet. I fail to see any grounds on which it might be claimed that another kind of imagination, or an imagination in any way hobbled or enfeebled produced in prose such figures as that in which Donne said of a prince:

> If he be a lion and live by prey, and waste among cedars and pines, and I a mole and scratch out my bed in the ground, happy in this that I cannot see him; if he be a butterfly the son of a silkworm, and I a scarab the seed of dirt; if he go to execution in a chariot, and I in a cart or by foot, where is the glorious advantage?

or that in which he described the length of a day in heaven:

> Methusalem, with all his hundreds of years, was but a mushroom of a night's growth, to this day, and all the four monarchies, with all their thousands of years, and all the powerful kings, and all the beautiful queens of this world, were but as a bed of flowers, some gathered at six, some at seven, some at eight, all in one morning, in respect of this day.

However, such a definition should not suggest that the collection of images is an entirely objective matter. Its actual application involves arbitrary decisions at several points. Thus, for instance, such a situation arises in every case where the figurative sense of a word or phrase is so conventionalized or faded with use that it is doubtful whether the writer was at all conscious of that sense. When, for example, Donne refers to "storms of persecution," the "jaws of hell," or the "root of sin," are these to be considered as drawn respectively from "weather," "animals," and "nature," and therefore indicative of interest in these sources, or are they used—as I think these particular phrases are—with virtually no feeling for their figurative backgrounds? The metaphors in such phrases seem almost as fossilized as those in "capricious," "disaster," "daisy," or any of the thousands of words in the language whose metaphoric origins have long since been forgotten. Although each of these images may be judged on its value for our purpose, the decision must often be personal. Fortunately, images of such doubtful figurative value are in any case of little importance as evidence, especially as compared with the large body of vivid and emphatic images which can be collected from the work of the average writer.

Once the collecting of images has been completed, similar decisions are necessary in the work of classification. I sought, of course, to avoid imposing such classifications from without, to allow them, instead, to grow out of those groupings into which they seemed naturally to fall; but even the broad "chapter" and "part" divisions at which I finally arrived called for the drawing of lines of demarcation, and, consequently, of occasional arbitrary classification. What follows will be better understood if I make clear not only where these occurred but how I sought to reduce this subjective element to a minimum.

The major problem is that raised by those knotty images which are composed of or include other images. Thus, when Donne says of the Earl of Somerset's bride,

> Then from these wombes of starres, the
> Brides bright eyes,
> At every glance, a constellation flyes,
> And sowes the Court with starres, and doth
> prevent
> In light and power, the all-ey'd firmament,

the figure, considered as a whole, utilizes images from "birth," "heavenly bodies," "farming," and "human characteristics." Although the "heavenly bodies" aspect seems to dominate, the other three categories are definitely drawn upon. The most objective solution was to classify the figure under all four categories and actually consider it as containing four separate metaphors. This is a multiple image; much more troublesome is the type which is essentially simple but draws upon or is in some way related to any one of several sources, sometimes depending upon the point of view adopted. Thus, a figure like that in which he describes a fawning court parasite as

> A thing more strange, than on Niles slime,
> > the Sunne
> E'r bred,

might be considered as drawing on "birth" or "animals"; while such a one as that in which he compares the world after Elizabeth Drury's death to

> a compassionate Turcoyse which doth tell
> By looking pale, the wearer is not well,

belongs, from one point of view, to "medicine," and from another, to "gems." The most satisfactory way out in such cases was to classify each image of this sort under the several headings suggested, but to consider it not as multiple, but as simple and single.*

Obviously the difficulty here arises from the fact that our classifications tend to fuse or overlap. This is as it should be. We are dealing with the volatile stuff of imagination, and although we can distinguish clearly between extremes among its representatives, anyone who under-

---

* I catalogued eighty-six such images; but none under more than two sources.

takes any comprehensive system of classification with such materials must here and there act arbitrarily. In the chapters that follow, this will be most evident, I think, in the distinctions made between such divisions as "Rivers and Seas" and "Sea Travel and Exploration," between "The Heavens" and "Ideas of the Universe," between the human types dealt with in "Men and Characteristics" and the common human types in the chapters dealing with special subjects. Although, from the point of view of source, there is, for example, a decided difference between an image that comes simply from gazing at the sea and one from the science of navigation, between one that comes from the sense of sunlight and one that issues from a complex theory in astronomy, and although, as we shall see, these divisions represent distinct imaginative tendencies, the actual drawing of lines between divisions occasionally necessitates summary disposal or equivocal cross-classifying.

These observations also hold true of my division of the entire body of Donne's images into three major parts. In Part I, I sought to bring together all those groups of figures which seemed to be drawn from books, science, and the arts—in short, from the whole world of learning; in Part II all those coming from daily life; and in Part III all those from the direct apprehension of the surrounding world of nature. Here, too, the process of division was suggested by the material itself and never carried out at the expense of any more obvious or significant unity in a special subject. Thus, although "Law Courts and Prisons" deals in part with ordinary prisoners, a type which might conceivably have been a subdivision of the chapter on "Men and Characteristics" in Part II, and although the more technical aspects of navigation (under "Sea Travel and Exploration" in Part II) might have been segregated and made into a separate chapter in Part I, I felt that such groups were natural units and would make for much more coherence and much less repetition if treated as such.

It was such decisions, and, what is more important, the consciousness that no two images are equally significant as evidence, that caused me some misgiving concerning the value of graphs or statistical tables of images. I have appended one such table, but only to indicate the scope of the investigation upon which my conclusions are based. A graph or image count used for any other purpose seems to me to put undue emphasis upon mere quantity and number, and to suggest that images are translatable into significant mathematical terms and formulae. It is sufficient if such a study as this serves as a prism to break up the light of a writer's imagery into its spectrum of colors; to attempt more is to break the butterfly on the wheel. Short of not classifying at all, the three major parts and the score of chapters into which I have divided the body of Donne's images represent as broad an approach as I could achieve.

THE EVIDENCE

PART I

III

IDEAS OF THE UNIVERSE

In 1543, with relatively little heralding or fanfare, the *De revolutionibus orbium coelestium* of Nicholas Copernicus was published by his disciple Rheticus, and lit a flame that was to explode into one of the most revolutionary of scientific doctrines and the most exciting intellectual heresy of the Renaissance. Reaching with the cosmic reach of astronomical calculation into the whirling maze of the Aristotelian-Ptolemaic universe, the Polish priest stopped the sun, eliminated a multitude of planetary movements, loosed the earth from its age-old anchorage at the centre of things, and flung it, rotating and revolving, into space.

When Copernicus died others—and notably such English scientists as John Dee, Robert Recorde, Thomas Digges, and William Gilbert *—picked up the torch he had lit, and carried it forward into those obscure places where the authority of Aristotle and Ptolemy still reigned absolute. But the final blow was not struck until Galileo brought to bear the direct observations of his magical "glass"—the telescope. In 1610, in his *Siderius Nuncius,* he published the results of his scrutinies of the skies and turned the torch of Copernicus into a veritable beacon that illuminated the new universe for all who had eyes to see and minds to accept.

A man who was possessed, like Donne, of an "hydroptique immoderate desire of humane learning," to use his own words, could hardly help following with the greatest

---

* See Francis R. Johnson's *Astronomical Thought in Renaissance England,* Baltimore, Johns Hopkins Press, 1937.

eagerness every step these revolutionaries of science were taking, and a poet who, like Donne, found in scientific fact the clarity, objectivity, and subtle distinctions most perfectly adapted to illuminating his feelings, could hardly help reflecting in his imagery almost every aspect of his reactions to the new philosophy.*

One point that should immediately be made concerning Donne's use of astronomy—or of any learning—is that he apparently took it for granted that imagery, so long as it fulfilled its essential function of clarifying and making vivid, might be drawn from any side of a controversial question. We may therefore expect that his images from astronomy will levy almost as freely on the Ptolemaic system as on the Copernican, and occasionally on both at once. In *Ignatius His Conclave* Donne introduces Copernicus as foremost among those who claim from Lucifer a place in hell, a place to which only they had title who had attempted such innovations as "gave an affront to all antiquitie, and induced doubts, and anxieties, and scruples, and . . . at length established opinions, directly contrary to all established before." [1] We will not be surprised, then, if Donne's imagery reflects not only this last conclusion but also all the preceding stages—that is, the old theories and the anxieties that accompanied the change to the new. To be sure, by the frequency with which certain attitudes are reflected, by the ideas to which images are attached, and even by the language in which they are couched, we may in most cases be able to decide what the writer's

---

* For those who wish to follow in detail Donne's responses to the astronomical discoveries of his time and to the new philosophy in general, Charles Monroe Coffin has provided a painstaking and carefully documented study in *John Donne and the New Philosophy* (Columbia University Press, New York, 1937).

[1] All numbered notes refer to Donne's own works and are to be found appended to the body of the text. The key to all abbreviated references to Donne's works may also be found there.

position really is.

The persistence in Donne's imagery of fragments from the Aristotelian-Ptolemaic vision and of much of its terminology of first movers, unchanging firmaments, and intelligences of spheres can be illustrated without difficulty. The *primum mobile* of Aristotle supplies the figure when Donne writes to Sir Henry Goodere that it is not true that "all mankinde hath but one soul, which informes and rules us all, as one Intelligence doth the firmament and all the Starres," [2] and when he observes in "Good Friday, 1613. Riding Westward,"

> Pleasure or businesse, so, our Soules admit
> For their first mover, and are whirld by it.
> Hence is't, that I am carryed towards the West
> This day, when my Soules forme bends toward
>   the East. [3]

The same poem opens with

> Let mans Soule be a Spheare, and then, in this
> The intelligence that moves, devotion is;

in another letter to Goodere he describes the uncertainties of a friendship which is not moved by the "proper intelligence, discretion," as characterized, like the lower spheres, by eccentricities, trepidations and deviations; [4] and in "The Extasie" he says:

> Our bodies why doe wee forbeare?
> They are ours, though they are not wee, Wee are
> The intelligences, they the spheares. [5]

Even when he assures his beloved, apropos of a fever, [6] that her beauty and entire being are "unchangeable firmament" —in which a burning fit is only a meteor, soon spent—he is making use of the basic Aristotelian conception of the heavens as beyond all change. Occasionally, too, there is a clear recall of the dizzyingly numerous concentric circles which characterized most Ptolemaic maps of planetary orbits. From this source come such pictures as that of love's additions as all concentric unto one point—the beloved; and that of the heavens, earth, cities and men as concentric unto decay.[7]

But these ideas are used neither vividly nor with the originality that betokens a really stimulated mind. The Ptolemaic system had long since become an ancient tradition disturbed only by occasional quibbles. Compared to these metaphors, almost any one of those that draws on Copernicism—the "new philosophy" as Donne calls it again and again—reveals all the doubt and wonder and excitement of a fired imagination, all the electric of intellectual disturbance. Thus in one extended image in the *Devotions Upon Emergent Occasions* there is mirrored in swift, almost bewildering succession, acceptance of the new ideas, perplexity and doubt in the face of them, and finally sullen, cavilling criticism. "I am up," cries Donne as he rises dizzily from a sickbed,

> and I seeme to stand, and I goe round; and I am a new Argument of the new Philosophie, That the Earth moves round; why may I not beleeve, that the whole earth moves in a round motion . . . when as I seeme to stand to my Company, and yet am carried, in a giddy, and circular motion . . .?[8]

This, even if fantastic, seems to be on the side of the new theory; but the fact that there are still two sides leads to confusion and to the skeptical comment—"Man hath no center but misery; there and onely there, hee is fixt, and sure to finde himselfe"; and this in turn to

> . . . as in the Heavens, there are but a few Circles,
> that goe about the whole world, but many Epicircles,
> and other lesser Circles . . . so of those men, which
> are raised, and put into Circles, few of them move
> from place to place . . . but fall into little Circles,
> and, within a step or two, are at their end, and not
> so well, as they were in the Center, from which they
> were raised.

This is a carping kind of criticism and since he adds,
"Everything serves to exemplifie, to illustrate mans misery," some might be tempted to argue that he had to find
some adverse comment on the new ideas if his parallel
was to be complete. To say, however, that he would thus
distort so vital a belief is to suggest that he was not ingenious enough to find a figure naturally appropriate.
Moreover, we have at least one other image which gives
expression to the same sullen type of acceptance. To dem-
onstrate how the Roman religion appeared to bring its
adherents nearer heaven while really carrying heaven ever
farther off, he compares it to

> Copernicisme in the Mathematiques [which] hath
> carried earth farther up, from the stupid Center;
> and yet not honoured it, nor advantaged it, because
> . . . it hath carried heaven so much higher from
> it. . . .[9]

In addition to this, we have, of course, the direct statement of "The First Anniversary" [10] with its almost de-
spairing cries of "new Philosophy calls all in doubt," "the
Sun is lost," and "freely men confesse that this world's
spent." *

It is in still another letter to Goodere—to whom he

---

* In Sermon 80 (A. III, 483) he again uses the new philosophy as
if its effect were disintegrative, and yet again with a kind of grudging
acceptance. "I need not call in new philosophy," he says, "that denies

seems to have addressed a major part of his observations
on the new science—that he adopts a figure using Copernicism without any taint of doubt:

> I often compare not you and me, but the sphear in
> which your resolutions are, and my wheel; both I
> hope concentrique to God: for methinks the new
> Astronomie is thus appliable well, that we which
> are a little earth, should rather move towards God,
> then that he . . . towards us.[11]

The image, using, and using accurately, the relationship
between the "wheel" or daily rotation of the earth and its
annual revolution, moves forward with a confidence that
suggests complete grasp of the facts involved.

The same assimilation is revealed when he writes to
Lady Bedford,

> As new Philosophy arrests the Sunne,
> And bids the passive earth about it runne,
> So wee have dull'd our minde, it hath no ends;
> Onely the bodie's busie, and pretends;[12]

and here, moreover, in such verbs as "arrest" and "bid,"
there enters a touch of grudging awe, an almost involun-
tary recall of the magic of Joshua stopping the sun in
Gibeon.* The same attitude is evident when he chooses the

---

a settledness, an acquiescence in the very body of the earth, but makes
the earth to move in that place, where we thought the sun had moved;
I need not that help, that the earth itself is in motion, to prove this, that
nothing upon earth is permanent . . ."

* Similarly, in *Ignatius His Conclave* (H. 359) he speaks of Galileo
as one "who of late hath summoned the other worlds, the Stars to come
neerer to him, and give him an account of themselves"; and Copernicus,
depicted as one made arrogant, almost blasphemous by his discoveries,
beats on the doors of hell and cries out to Lucifer (H. 363-364):

> Are these shut against me, to whom all the Heavens were ever
> open, who was a Soule to the Earth, and gave it motion? . . .
> I am he, which pitying thee who wert thrust into the Center of
> the world, raysed both thee, and thy prison, the Earth, up into the
> Heavens . . . who have turned the whole frame of the world,
> and am thereby almost a new Creator . . .

raising of the earth into the heavens by certain "late philosophers" as the only earthly wonder capable of imaging the miracle of resurrection.[13]

But the full impact of these dislocations, of a world shaken literally out of joint, can be felt most sharply in such a figure as he invokes to bring home to men the effect of young Prince Henry's death:

> If then least moving of the center, make
> More, then if whole hell belch'd, the world to
> shake,
> What must this do, centers distracted so,
> That wee see not what to beleeve or know?[14]

and in that passage where he adds another image to that wonderfully subtle series in "A Valediction: forbidding mourning" defining exactly how undemonstrative need be a temporary parting between true lovers:

> Moving of th'earth brings harmes and feares,
> Men reckon what it did and meant,
> But trepidation of the spheares,
> Though greater farre, is innocent,[15]

a figure which is by way of being a summary of almost all that we have just considered. The first two lines allude to the almost superstitious fears, to all the wonder and excited speculation stirred up by the shifting of the earth; and the last two to a moving which took place in one of the spheres of the old system, a movement which, for all that it may have been greater, was, Donne says, innocent— innocent only, one suspects, of revolutionary implications.

When we find, in addition to these images, such a direct statement as that in *Biathanatos* where Donne calls all remaining Aristotelians "pertinacious" and "stubborn" because they still maintain the inalterability of the heavens, "though by many experiences of new Stars, the reason which moved Aristotle seems now to be utterly defeated," [16] it is clear that Donne was ready to accept the new philosophy, and retained fragments of the old system only in so far as they were poetically useful.

One of the most exciting aspects of the exploration of the skies was the use of the telescope and the discovery of new stars. Year after year Kepler and Galileo agitated Europe with announcements of the new sidereal bodies they had caught in the far-flung nets of their "optick glasses." The awe with which men received these announcements—the sense of cosmic mysteries audaciously pierced and the strange things that might ensue—is repeatedly reflected in Donne's images. "Bee thou a new starre," he exhorted Lady Elizabeth,

> that to us portends
> Ends of much wonder. . . .[17]

and, seeking as ever new metaphors in which to couch his panegyrics, he uses a vivid distinction between stars and comets to point up the difference between innocent women and those actively good:

> Who vagrant transitory Comets sees,
>   Wonders, because they'are rare; But a
>   new starre
> Whose motion with the firmament agrees,
>   Is miracle; for, there no new things are;
>
> In woman so perchance milde innocence
>   A seldome comet is, but active good
> A miracle, which reason scapes, and sense.[18]

Comets may be rare and wonderful, he says here, but new stars are nothing short of miraculous. And miraculous, it should be noted, is the word with which the laymen of every age express their awe in the presence of any great scientific achievement.

Only the clergy, it appears, are more powerful than these astronomers when it comes to acting as intermediaries between God and man. If astronomers using "opticks" bring a "new-found Starre" to us, Donne exclaims, how brave are they who can "bring man to heaven, and heaven againe to man." [19] The "new-found Starre" here is the counterpart of the "new-found-land" of contemporary exploration by land and water. That Donne was entirely conscious of the parallel between the explorers of sky and of earth is made even clearer when he writes in a verse letter:

> We'have added to the world Virginia, 'and sent
> Two new starres lately to the firmament.[20]

The fact that the two stars lately sent to the firmament may refer to two noble friends who had died a short time before * makes his admiration of the scientists seem even greater, attributing to them the power to put stars in heaven as God puts the souls of men there.

The interest with which he followed the writings and activities of the astronomers is revealed in another way in those images which utilize curious speculation concerning the actual procedure of the star-gazers. Thus, young Elizabeth Drury died while men debated who should have her—

> as when heaven lookes on us with new eyes,
> Those new starres every Artist exercise,
> What place they should assigne to them they
> doubt,
> Argue, 'and agree not, till those starres goe out.[21]

Similarly, to describe the age of the men of biblical times he can say only that it is so great that

---

* See Herbert J. C. Grierson, *The Poems of John Donne*, Oxford, 1912, II, 132; hereafter designated as *Grierson*.

> . . . if a slow pac'd starre had stolne away
> From the observers marking, he might stay
> Two or three hundred yeares to see't againe,
> And then make up his observation plaine.[22]

Here is one place where any number of images might have served his purpose; the choice of astronomy is all the more significant.

If we mention in addition to these a few metaphors which make use of the galaxy as described by Galileo, particularly of its whiteness, its infinity of stars, and their minor magnitude,[23] we have dealt with the great majority of those figures in Donne that stem directly from one of the most important movements in the science and philosophy of his time.

*   *

So far we have considered only those images which seemed to have some bearing on the new astronomy or on the contrast of the old science with the new. Turning to those which deal with stars as stars—apart, that is, from scientific movements, the first thing we note is the repeated use Donne makes of their reliance upon the sun as the source of all light.[24] As mere reflections they are subject to its coming and going; and this is the source, for example, of the parallel in Paradoxe XII between the exact way in which virginity is taken away by marriage and the subtle supplanting of the light of the stars by that of the sun.[25] That appears in the prose; an even more precise observation of this type becomes the sensitive integral stuff of poetry when he declares to his beloved:

> And yet no greater, but more eminent,
>   Love by the Spring is growne;
>   As, in the firmament,
> Starres by the Sunne are not inlarg'd, but
>   showne.[26]

Among the other heavenly phenomena that attract
Donne falling stars are prominent. The enigma of their
sudden passage and abrupt disappearance earns them their
position as initial symbol of the impossible in the famous
song, "Goe, and catche a falling starre." In the epithalamion for Lord Somerset, the bridegroom, hurrying to the
bedded bride, is compared to one who, seeing a star fall,

> runs apace,
> And findes a gellie in the place.[27]

Though quaint to us, the notion of a falling star turning
to jelly was, as Professor Grierson points out,* a common
one. The startling swiftness of such a star alone of
natural phenomena seems capable of suggesting the quite
inexpressible speed of an unfettered soul; compared with
such a soul, Donne declares, even these falling stars are
"slow pac'd." [28]

Surrounded by much the same aura of mystery are
lightning, eclipses, meteors and comets. Twice, in the
same words, Donne compares the life of one who gives no
thought to the reason for his existence with lightning,
whose beginning and end, says Donne, no one knows.[29]
Although he understood eclipses, he used them, as he did
all obscurings of vital light, as symbolic of misfortune and
affliction.[30] In accordance with this he makes the earth—
ordinarily a mere recipient of light, and, in lunar eclipses,
that which actually cuts it off—stand for ignorance in one
place, and in another for the human body dragging down
the mind.[31] Meteors, too, seemed to have interested him
because of one particular characteristic—their apparent
hovering or suspension between heaven and earth. This
serves to figure forth with almost equal aptness such a

---

* *Grierson,* II, 97-98.

remarkable variety of things as the position of angels, of bishops, a sick man near death, man's life as it is divided between the here and the hereafter, and Jesuits who gaze toward heaven as they conspire on earth.[32] It is true that in several places he uses them because they "cause talk" or are of an "ominous and incendiarie presaging"; [33] it is to comets, however, that he attributes real influence over the fates of men. They create fear and perhaps even rebellions. Because of the fact that no almanac predicts when one will break out and "no Astrologer tels us when the effects will be accomplished" they serve Donne's purpose throughout that "Meditation" in which he considers how his illness stole upon him insidiously and without warning.[34]

Entirely indebted to the pseudo-science of astrology is the passage in "A Valediction: of my name, in the window" in which Donne urges his beloved to treasure that scratched memento because it contains all the love and grief which were rife when it was cut. It contains their influence, not symbolically, but actually;

> As all the vertuous powers which are
> Fix'd in the starres, are said to flow
> Into such characters, as graved bee
> When these starres have supremacie.[35]

Notwithstanding these instances and those few that make use of the divisions of the zodiac, or the word "lunatic" in its original sense, the admixture of astrology in these images is not considerable.* The old and elaborate system whereby men found a veritable network of affinities between the affairs of human beings and the heavenly

---

* Professor Grierson (II, 108-109) draws attention to Donne's allusion to "drawing forth heavens Scheme" (in Satyre I, l. 60), but even this reference is mocking in attitude; the poet attributes the practice to a "gulling weather Spie."

bodies, and concerning which most Elizabethans were almost as superstitious as the men of earlier ages, finds little reflection in Donne. In this direction, at least, Donne's debt to medieval thought is at a minimum.

THE FOUR ELEMENTS

Closely allied to the Ptolemaic conception of the planetary system, and destined to accompany it into the limbo of discarded doctrines, was the theory that the universe is made up of four elements. Aristotle, following more ancient writers, held that there were four fundamental qualities, hot, cold, wet, and dry, and that these met in binary combinations to produce the four elements; these, listed according to the supposed order of their densities, were earth, water, air, and fire. This neat gradation from density to rarity, although superficial, was useful, and it repeatedly finds place in Donne's imagery.

In "The Dissolution," which plays in the most fanciful vein with several aspects of the theory, Donne is the disappointed lover, made up of the

> fire of Passion, sighes of ayre,
> Water of tears, and earthly sad despaire.[36]

It is a convenient gradation which lends a neat cumulative effect to the listing of his emotions. The theory held, moreover, that the celestial regions must consist of fire, the element of least density, as contrasted with earth, which was considered gross and drossy. This is the background of Donne's metaphor when he asserts that the love of a woman like Lady Huntingdon gives off such light and heat as would

> force us thither to intend,
> But soule we finde too earthly to ascend;

and, again:

> No more can impure man retaine and move
> In that pure region of worthy love:
> Then earthly substance can unforc'd aspire,
> And leave his nature to converse with fire.[37]

If fire and air are the sheerest and purest of the elements, we may expect that they will be made to serve in descriptions of Elizabeth Drury: they may be the finest of the elements but next to her they are, Donne says in the typically extravagant strain of the "Anniversaries," "thick grosse bodies." [38] It is the kind of figure George Puttenham was probably thinking of when in his *The Arte of English Poesie* he listed among the figures of speech "Hyperbole or the Over reacher, otherwise called the loud lyer."

Another phase of the same theory seems to be utilized when Donne laments that court, country, and city each makes a specialty of either pride, lust, or covetousness, and at the same time includes something of all three,

> As in the first Chaos confusedly
> Each elements qualities were in the'other three; [39]

and again—comparing the groping love of the first men with order emerging from original Chaos—

> Water declin'd with earth, the ayre did stay,
> Fire rose, and each from other but unty'd,
> Themselves unprison'd were and purify'd:
> So was love, first in vast confusion hid,
> An unripe willingnesse which nothing did,
> A thirst, an Appetite which had no ease,
> That found a want, but knew not what
>   would please.[40]

The source of all this is obviously that vision of the first Chaos as a disorder wherein each element had not yet disentangled itself, achieved purity, and undertaken its proper function. But what is perhaps the most interesting figure from this source occurs in the eloquent sermon which Donne preached at the funeral of Sir William Cokayne. Discoursing on that most pervasive of Elizabethan themes, the impermanence of earthly things, he illuminates it with a vision of elements never at rest:

> In the elements themselves, of which all sub-elementary things are composed, there is no acquiescence, but a vicissitudinary transmutation into one another; air condensed becomes water, a more solid body, and air rarefied becomes fire, a body more disputable, and inapparent. It is so in the condition of men too; a merchant condensed, kneaded and packed up in a great estate, becomes a lord; and a merchant rarefied, blown up by a perfidious factor, or by a riotous son, evaporates into air, into nothing, and is not seen.

The usefulness of all this material for Donne was apparently unimpaired by the fact that, along with the basic Ptolemaic doctrine, the theory of the elements—and especially that element of fire which was supposed to make up the celestial regions—was already undermined. The new philosophy "calls all in doubt," Donne himself had declared, and, as first example of its devasting effect,

The Element of fire is quite put out.[42]

THE UNIVERSE IN MAN

Another traditional concept utilized by Donne is that of man as a little world, a replica, in small, of the cosmos.

This notion of the external universe as macrocosm and man as microcosm goes back, of course, to antiquity; eventually, however, it became part of the neo-Platonic tradition, and in the sixteenth century, Paracelsus—whose doctrines Donne often refers to—made it a central point in an entire system of philosophy. The analogy, always considered instructive, suggests to Donne a variety of provocative parallels. An image referring directly to the theory occurs when he speaks of Elizabeth Drury as

> She to whom this world must it selfe refer,
> As Suburbs, or the Microcosme of her.[43]

Less direct but obviously stemming from the same source are such figures as

> I am a little world made cunningly
> Of Elements. . . .[44]

and,

> The soule with body, is a heaven combin'd
> with earth. . . .[45]

That he pondered the idea often and that it seemed always to yield something new and profitable is suggested when he writes: 'Stil when we return to that Meditation, that Man is a World, we find new discoveries."[46] In that world, he adds, man "him self will be the land, and misery the sea. . . ." To this opposition between land and sea—with the latter as the evil principle—he recurs on several occasions. In the last passage the sea was identified with misery; in the "Elegie on the Lady Marckham,"

> Man is the World, and death th'Ocean,
> To which God gives the lower parts of man;[47]

and, in Satyre V, as a third variation,

> . . . man is a world; in which, Officers
> Are the vast ravishing seas. . . .[48]

However, the most vivid images from this source seem to me to be those in which Donne builds up the basic parallel between macrocosm and microcosm with vital analogies issuing from direct experiences of the surrounding world. Two arresting examples occur in the *Meditations*. "Is this the honour which Man hath by being a litle world," he asks in his illness,

> That he hath these earthquakes in him selfe, sodaine shakings; these lightning, sodaine flashes; these thunders, sodaine noises; these Eclypses, sodain offuscations, and darknings of his senses; these Blazing stars, sodaine fiery exhalations; these Rivers of blood, sodaine red waters? [49]

and in another passage:

> If all the Veines in our bodies, were extended to Rivers, and all the Sinewes, to Vaines of Mines, and all the Muscles, that lye upon one another, to Hilles, and all the Bones to Quarries of stones, and all the other pieces, to the proportion of those which correspond to them in the world, the Aire would be too litle for this Orbe of Man to move in, the firmament would bee but enough for this Starre. . . . [50]

In such figures the rather remote macrocosm-microcosm idea is on the way to becoming a parallel between man and very immediate natural phenomena; but although there is some use of direct perceptions of the world of nature, the source of the image is still essentially a theory of bookish origin.

*　　*

Having determined the extent and nature of Donne's imaginative interest in ideas of the universe, something still remains to be said concerning the effect in his writing of imagery drawn from such a source. Although we are hardly prepared at this point to come to definitive conclusions, several are already manifest. The clearest of these is that such figures serve in his verse and prose to translate his feelings and states of mind into precise and objective terms—terms, one might say, characteristic of science. Whether he is talking of his beloved, his sicknesses, the death of friends or his relation to God, cosmographic theory is made to clarify and heighten meaning. Again and again emotional attitudes and things of the spirit are transmuted into the dispassionate terms of these scientific concepts. What we begin to see here is the part that imagery plays in what Donne critics have referred to as his intellectualizing of feeling.

Already apparent, too, is his tendency in the direction of images from ideas which were, even in his day, fairly recondite. Observing his utilization of these it is evident that he selects them not out of vanity or eccentricity but because they provide him with parallels which are peculiarly exact, sufficiently complex for his purposes, and unstaled by use. It is by virtue of such figures that he achieves freshness and impact, surprising and stimulating the reader into an awareness of his meaning that no stereotyped or faded figure could hope to provoke.

IV

MEDICINE AND ALCHEMY

Burdened with many old traditions and beset with the usual abundance of passing fetishes, Elizabethan-Jacobean medicine is a confusion of science, error, and charlatanism. In one and the same period, the great Harvey demonstrated the circulation of the blood, the insane were treated by scourging, and John Dee (abetted by Queen Elizabeth herself) conducted the most notorious of alchemical quests for the "elixir of life." With science already on the first step of the ladder but with medieval notions still prevalent, even enlightened Elizabethans were frequently guilty of the most flagrant inconsistencies of attitude.

In any case, each of these currents of theory and several others, too, are represented, even if only fragmentarily, in Donne's imagery. In fact, when Mary Paton Ramsay sought to identify the medieval doctrines in Donne's medical lore she found strands of neo-Platonism, cabalistic theosophy, alchemy, magic healing, and astrology *—a confusing picture, but a logical result of the fact that Donne had no occasion to subscribe to any one approach and many on which to make use of fragments from various approaches.

In the realm of general medicine, ancient writers, using the analogy of the four elements, earth, water, air, and fire, and their origin in the four fundamental qualities, dry, wet, cold, and hot, had developed the theory that basically

---

* *Les Doctrines Médiévales chez Donne, Le Poète Métaphysicien de L'Angleterre,* Oxford University Press, 1917, Ch. VI, "Des 'Sciences'".

the health of the body is dependent on four humours, blood, phlegm, back bile, and yellow bile (or choler). Ill health, they said, was the result of a defect or excess in any one of these humours. This notion appears in Donne's imagery when, for example, referring to alleged irregularities in Sir Henry Goodere's religious belief, he writes: "I am angry, that any should think, you had in your Religion peccant humours, defective, or abundant . . ." [1] and when, in *Ignatius His Conclave,* he makes Ignatius challenge the practicality of the theological doctrines of Philip Nerius thus: "In what Kingdome have they corrected these humours, which offend the Pope, either by their Incision or cauterising?" [2] It was a Galenist doctrine that such a disproportion should be corrected by the addition of decoctions of herbs which would oppose hot with cold, wet with dry, and so on. Paracelsus had jettisoned this entire system, contending that each disease is caused by some bad essence which must be purged chemically. It is this disagreement which lies behind the image when Donne writes to Sir Henry Wotton:

> Onely'in this one thing, be no Galenist: To make
> Courts hot ambitions wholesome, do not take
> A dramme of Countries dulnesse; do not adde
> Correctives, but as chymiques, purge the bad. [3]

Other aspects of the conception of body humours and their proportions appear in several images utilizing leachers or the practice of bleeding, as, for instance, when he says that Ireland is suffering from an ague of wars,

> Which time will cure: yet it must doe her good
> If she were purg'd, and her head vayne let blood. [4]

Since, however, the theory of humours was an exceedingly popular one among Elizabethans in general, these few images indicate, if anything, no extraordinary interest on Donne's part. On the other hand, we find a provocative number of images traceable to the somewhat more remote influence of the tradition of Paracelsus, radical sixteenth century German-Swiss physician and alchemist. The curious thing about this is that Donne's direct references to Paracelsus are derogatory—except for one which alludes to him as an "excellent Chirurgian." [5] He asserts that Paracelsus has received too much credit for his work,[6] mocks the pompous name he used—Philippus Aureolus Theophrastus Paracelsus Bombast of Hohenheim, and in *Ignatius His Conclave*, where the physician-alchemist is ranked with Copernicus among the revolutionary challengers of established doctrine, he makes him say of himself:

> . . . I broght all Methodicall Phisitians, and the art it selfe into so much contempt, that that kind of phisick is almost lost; This also was ever my principal purpose, that no certaine new Art, nor fixed rules might be established, but that al remedies might be dangerously drawne from my uncertaine, ragged, and unperfect experiments, in triall whereof, how many men have been made carkases?

and again:

> . . . whereas almost all poysons are so disposed and conditioned by nature, that they offend some of the senses, and so are easily discerned and avoided, I brought it to passe, that that trecherous quality of theirs might bee removed, and so they might safely bee given without suspicion, and yet performe their office as strongly.[7]

Moreover, it was undoubtedly the fact that Paracelsus had discarded the conventional humours for three alchemical elements, mercury, sulphur, and salt, that lay behind Donne's plaintive comment in "The Second Anniversary":

> Have not all soules thought
> For many ages, that our body'is wrought
> Of Ayre, and Fire, and other Elements?
> And now they thinke of new ingredients,
> And one Soule thinkes one, and another way
> Another thinkes, and 'tis an even lay.[8]

Despite all this, and very much in the same way that he had utilized—as if fascinated almost against his will—the disturbing doctrines of Copernicus, Donne draws again and again upon Paracelsian theory. I have already quoted the image in which he clearly contrasts the basic Paracelsian and Galenist attitudes; but it is the Paracelsian notion of a "natural body balm" which catches his fancy most often. According to this belief, there was present in the human body a natural force which preserved it in health and cured it in illness.* To this mystic agent, called balm or balsamum, Donne refers again and again. Naturally it proved particularly useful in figures eulogizing patrons; in one form or another he applied it to Lady Bedford, Elizabeth Drury, and Lord Harrington. To the first he wrote:

> In everything there naturally growes
> A Balsamum to keepe it fresh, and new,
> It'were not injur'd by extrinsique blowes
> Your birth and beauty are this Balme in you;[9]

and of the second and the effect of her death on the world:

> Sicke World . . . since shee
> Thy'intrinsique balme, and thy preservative,
> Can never be renew'd. . . .[10]

---

* J. M. Stillman, *Paracelsus,* Chicago, Open Court Publishing Co., 1920, p. 60.

It is interesting to note that when he turns to the same theory in prose, the only difference is a tendency to expand, to present fully, to abandon the strict economy and ellipses that mark his poetry. Thus he writes in a sermon:

> Now physicians say, That man hath in his constitution, in his complexion, a natural virtue, which they call *Balsamum suum*, His own balsamum, by which any wound which a man could receive in his body would cure itself, if it could be kept clean from the annoyances of the air, and all extrinsic incumbrances. Something that hath some proportion and analogy to this balsamum of the body, there is in the soul of man too: the soul hath . . . spikenard, a perfume, a fragrancy, a sweet savour in herself. For . . . virtuous inclinations, and a disposition to moral goodness, is more natural to the soul of man . . . than health is to the body; [11]

and in another, meant to prove the superior energy of moral evil—

> If a man do but prick a finger, and bind it over that part, so that the spirits, or that which they call the balsamum of the body, cannot descend, by reason of that ligature, to that part, it will gangrene . . . which is an argument, and an evidence, that mischiefs are more operative . . . than remedies. . . . [12]

In the latter example an analogy becomes a proof in itself, a form of reasoning which lay at the bottom of all too many of the false conclusions of medieval science. Finally, pursuing the balsamum theory even further, and using the result to illustrate how the truly virtuous are equally so in all things, Donne writes to a friend:

>The later Physicians says, that when our naturall
>inborn preservative is corrupted or wasted, and
>must be restored by a like extracted from other
>bodies; the chief care is that the Mummy have in
>it no excelling quality, but an equally digested
>temper: And such is true vertue.[13]

Almost as frequent in Donne's imagery as the idea of
a body balm is that of the popular procedure of purging.
When Donne describes Cabal as the "Paracelsian physic
of the understanding," [14] or when, extolling the catharsis
in spiritual suffering, he writes that these

>for extracted chimique medicine serve,
>And cure much better, and as well preserve;
>Then are you your own physicke, or need none,
>When Still'd, or purg'd by tribulation,[15]

he is apparently thinking of the practice as part of the
Paracelsian contention that each disease is caused by a
bad essence which must be purged chemically. Probably
the most fantastic analogy to issue from this source is
that between the way God can use scandals and tempta-
tions to physic the spirit of man and the way apothecaries
mix vipers and poisons to make "sovereign treacles." [16]

I have referred to the passage wherein Donne speaks
favorably of Paracelsus; in that same passage we find
what seems to be an acceptance of Paracelsus' belief in
the efficacy of talismans. Whether or not he really accepted this motion, it prepares us for the image he uses
when he compares the enervation of the world after Elizabeth Drury's death to

>a compassionate Turcoyse which doth tell
>By looking pale, the wearer is not well,[17]

or when, in another place, he utilizes a fancied medicinal
quality in pearls.[18] In sharp contrast to these is the meta-

phor put into the mouth of Ignatius when, still attacking the theological opinions of Philip Nerius as impractical, he exclaims: "Do they hope to cure their diseases, by talking and preaching, as it were with charmes and enchantments?" [19] Apparently there is little need for consistency when different attitudes or seemingly conflicting beliefs serve equally well for the purposes of imaginative illustration.

Among the other fragments of theory attributable to the influence of the Paracelsian tradition are those in images making use of bezoar, opium or medicinal baths. The first, a substance found in the stomachs of herbivorous animals, is typical of the more curious sources of Donne's imagery. Because it is first a mere concretion in an animal, then passes to the apothecary, and at last to its work in the human body, it serves in one instance to illustrate salvation in decree, in Christ's death, and finally in application among men; and in another instance—a totally different idea—the way the destitute are helped even by the refuse of servants.[20] It appears in connection with these destitute ones when Donne says in Meditation 7 that their greatest sickness is hunger, that to them

> ordinary porridge would bee Julip enough, the refuse of our servants, Bezar enough, and the off-scouring of our Kitchen tables, Cordiall enough.[21]

The application of such a limited idea, or aspects of it, to a variety of statements of meaning is not unusual; it suggests that a writer's interests so govern his choice of images that he may insist on finding illustrative or metaphoric uses for those interests, discovering significances in them which might never occur to another.

From the allied work of apothecary, simplicist, and

herbalist comes a small but impressively remote-sounding group of images. None, however, is detailed. Typical is the comparison between religious disputers or cavillers and simplicists who "know the venom and peccant quality of every herb, but cannot fit them to medicine"; [22] or between the well-stocked drugs of apothecaries' shops and the numerous and easily dispensed indulgences of the Jesuits. [23] Of drugs in general Donne in other figures utilizes plantain and amber, the cathartic aspects of rhubarb and aloes, the sweetening effect of julep, and the stimulation of cordials.

Obviously appropriate for making clear the virtues of his numerous patron-friends are the various general remedies popular in Elizabethan medicine. Lady Bedford's attributes comprise a mithridate, the perfect electuary against all and sundry poisons; [24] and Elizabeth Drury's are so wonderfully fused that no one of them can be said to excel,

> as in Mithridate, or just perfumes,
> Where all good things being met, no one
> presumes
> To governe, or to triumph on the rest,
> Only because all were, no part was best. [25]

All in all, Donne finds imaginative use for a considerable variety of ailments and treatments, both common and uncommon. Among the ailments we find the jerking and shaking of ague, the swollen heaviness of dropsy, the rotting of gangrene, the lingering of consumption, the riddling power of the pox, the fever in calenture, and obvious aspects of leprosy, the vapors, apoplexy (and its effect, "lethargy"), plague, rheum, and scurvy; among the treatments, besides those already considered, appear cauterizing, fomenting, salves and plasters, and, for madmen, scourging. However, none of these is utilized with any degree of elaboration, and only ague, dropsy, and gangrene, appear repeatedly. The first of these serves in one place to figure the fitfulness of spasmodic religious devotion; in another, uncertain love; and in a third, alternating war and peace.[26] In the well-known verse letter, "The Storme," the sailors note

> the ships sicknesses, the Mast
> Shak'd with this ague, and the Hold and Wast
> With a salt dropsie clog'd. . . .[27]

and in "The Litany" the poet gives voice to the hope that

> This intermitting aguish Pietie;
> That snatching cramps of wickednesse
> And Apoplexies of fast sin, may die.[28]

Dropsy, when it occurs in the form "hydroptic," signifying an extreme degree of absorptiveness, is used to epitomize avarice, a drunkard's thirst, or, most interesting of all, the "immoderate desire of humane learning and languages" that characterized Donne himself.[29]

* *

Of the several divisions into which Donne's images from medicine fall, those connected with anatomy and surgery make up the largest and most unified group. The work of Vesalius in the sixteenth century had sent anatomy far ahead of other branches of medicine, and although in some quarters dissection was still considered impious, demonstrations were held at regular intervals by the Barber Surgeons Company and by licensed individuals. It is probable that Donne had ample opportunity to witness such demonstrations; and his imagery suggests that he may have supplemented such observations with reading.

The term "anatomy" occurs frequently in the literature of the period, either in the sense of dissection or analysis—as in such familiar titles as the *Anatomie of Absurditie, The Anatomy of Melancholy,* and Donne's own "An Anatomie of the World"—or, less often, in the sense of a dissected corpse or a skeleton. It occurs in this latter sense, together with the rarer word "skeleton" itself, when Ignatius in *Ignatius His Conclave* charges that the theological doctrines of Philip Nerius were like those of a theorist in medicine—never applied, never made practical: ". . . what state," he asks, "have they cut into an Anatomy? what Sceleton have they provided for the instruction of Posterity?" [30] It is an interesting recognition of the value of dissection. A parallel respect for the practitioners themselves is revealed in such figures as

> You may as well call him an anatomist, that knows how to pare a nail, or cut a corn, or him a surgeon, that knows how to cut, and curl hair, as allow him understanding, that knows how to gather riches, or how to buy an office. . . .[31]

or when he compares God's piercing our souls and causing us to know ourselves better with the way a surgeon's anatomizings improve our understanding of our bodies.[32] Closer to the actual practice of the time is the analogy his imagination turns to when he says that he cannot continue too long his anatomy of that dead world which Elizabeth Drury left behind her because,

> as in cutting up a man that's dead,
> The body will not last out, to have read
> On every part, and therefore men direct
> Their speech to parts, that are of most effect.[33]

One is reminded of Sir Francis Bacon's fatal attempt to preserve such a body by refrigeration—even as is done today. Out of the same material comes the image with which

Donne refers to the signature which he has scratched for
his beloved on a window pane. Think, he says,

> this ragged bony name to bee
> My ruinous Anatomie.[34]

In those scratched outlines he sees a skeleton, and, in that,
another symbol of the mortality of men in general and
lovers in particular.

Although interesting, these involve no peculiar knowledge of the subject; in the several that follow we get really
recondite aspects of anatomy utilized confidently, if
strangely. In one, a striking figure, he undertakes to describe the flight of Elizabeth Drury's soul heavenward
through the spheres. Such is its speed, he says, that the
spheres, like strung beads, are at once many and one, and,

> As doth the pith, which, lest our bodies slacke,
> Strings fast the little bones of necke, and backe;
> So by the Soule doth death string Heaven
> and Earth.[35]

The other, suggested by the appearance of the human skull
—elsewhere referred to as a "deathshead"—is one of the
most macabre and gnarled of Donne's figures. Exhorting
men to purge evil from their thoughts by accepting spiritual burdens as Christ accepted the cross, he says:

> And as the braine through bony walls doth vent
> By sutures, which a Crosses forme present,
> So when thy braine workes, ere thou utter it,
> Crosse and correct concupiscence of witt.[36]

Study, however, will reveal it to be as precise as it is
obviously bizarre. In prose he goes even further, intro-
ducing—in a discussion of church schisms—a figure
couched in the Latin jargon of medical men; in it he

speaks of such schisms as *solutionem continui*—in lay language, the division of parts caused by wounds.[37] In the esoteric nature of such material, in its complexity, and in the technical precision of the parallels, we see at least one phase of the reason why Donne's verse is said to appeal to the intellect, why it is considered as much a cerebral as an emotional experience. Of course, if indulged in for their own sake, such images become merely virtuosity, a display wherein the setting of poetic statement outshines the gem itself; controlled, moulded to purpose, they become unique illuminations of meaning.

One other circumstance in the practice of Elizabethan anatomy made its contribution to Donne's imagery: although they had so far broken through church opposition as to perform dissections, the Barber Surgeons were still limited to using the bodies of executed criminals. This enters into several of the poet's figures; deriding Coryat's *Crudities,* he says:

> Worst malefactors . . .
> Do publike good, cut in Anatomies;
> So will thy booke in peeces;[38]

and, in "Loves Exchange," to the lover who tortures him:

> Kill, and dissect me, Love; for this
> Torture against thine owne end is,
> Rack't carcasses make ill Anatomies.[39]

THE ALCHEMICAL QUEST

Out of the theory that a perfect proportion of the elements in the human body meant health and that such a proportion could be induced arose the search for some universal medicine that would solve all the problems of physical life. In the hands of alchemists like Paracelsus it had become the quest for a panacea variously known as the quintessence, *elixir vitae,* and *aurum potabile,* the golden drink. By analogy it was supposed that the elixir could bring about proportion in metals, too, and that when the elements were thus perfectly combined in a base metal, it became gold. When gold-making rather than health was the end, the elixir was called the Philosopher's Stone, and was, by Donne's time, the goal of most alchemists. Ben Jonson's *The Alchemist* provides, of course, a classic example of the way in which charlatans, through gullible clients, could make alchemy a true way to gold—without benefit of *lapis philosophorum.*

The entire subject attracted Donne and he drew many vivid images from both streams of the pursuit. Prominent in the search for a sovereign remedy was the attempt to extract a quintessence, that is, a fifth essence or element, by the most intense purification of natural substances. Donne turns to this when he writes:

> But if this medicine, love, which cures all
> sorrow
> With more, not onely bee no quintessence,
> But mixt of all stuffes, paining soule, or sense,
>
> . . .
>
> Love's not so pure, and abstract as they use
> To say. . . .[40]

and again, in "A Nocturnall upon S. Lucies Day":

> For I am every dead thing,
> In whom love wrought new Alchimie.
> For his art did expresse
> A quintessence even from nothingnesse.[41]

What is apparently a similar procedure is utilized when Donne says that virtue comes most easily in the retiredness of home, as physicians

> when they would infuse
> Into any'oyle, the Soules of Simples, use
> Places, where they may lie still warme, to
> chuse;[42]

and in prose, when he speaks of the cabalists as having a "theological alchymy to draw sovereign tinctures and spirits from plain and gross literal matter." [43]

In general, alchemy and its chief instrument, the limbeck seem to occur to Donne when he is seeking something to symbolize a process of thoroughgoing purification and refinement. Such, he says, was the effect of many schools and courts on Sir Henry Wotton's personality, such was Elizabeth Drury's transformation of ordinary feminine characteristics, and such was death to Lady Marckham.[44] Moreover, since limbecks are narrow and crooked, they aptly describe the way God refines man by subjecting him to tribulation.[45]

In Donne's imagery, however, as in the life of his time, the alchemy of the gold-seekers dominates. He recurs again and again to the practitioners themselves and to their strange theories and fantastic practices. Once, in a metaphor occurring in a letter written during a stop at Plymouth, he refers directly to a contemporary alchemist, one whose reputation—or notoriety—was exceeded only by John Dee's. "I do not think," he writes, "that 77 Kelleys could distill 10 1. out of all the towne." [46] And elsewhere, for the length of a single long figure, he rivals Jonson in the use of the argot of the experimenters:

> Therefore David who was metal tried seven times in the fire, and desired to be such gold as might be laid up in God's treasury, might consider, that in the transmutation of metals, it is not enough to come to a calcination, or a liquefaction of the metal . . . nor to an ablution, to sever dross from

pure, nor to a transmutation, to make it a better
metal, but there must be a fixion, a settling there-
of, so that it shall not evaporate into nothing, nor
return to his former state. Therefore he saw that
he needed not only a liquefaction, a melting into
tears, nor only an ablution, and a transmutation,
those he had by this purging and this washing . . .
but he needed *fixionem,* an establishment. . . .[47]

It is curious to find such a passage as this, with its mumbo-
jumbo of charlatanism, in a sermon. His other applica-
tions of alchemy to religion are a little more congruous:
in one he describes the Catholics as looking upon a change
from Protestantism to their religion as an alchemical sub-
limation of copper into gold,[48] and in another he speaks
of God, who can change all men, as the true transmitter
of metals.[49]

One of the simplest and most effective of Donne's alchemical images in verse occurs in the dedication of his
"Holy Sonnets" to the Earl of Dorset. "I choose your
judgement," he writes to the Earl,

> As fire these drossie Rymes to purifie,
>   Or as Elixar, to change them to gold;
> You are that Alchimist which alwaies had
> Wit, whose one spark could make good things
>   of bad.[50]

Somewhat more fragmentary are those figures in which he
makes use of the distinction between the superficiality of
gilding or "informing" as compared with the thoroughness of complete transubstantiation. Speaking of Virtue,
he writes to the Countess of Huntingdon:

> She guilded us: But you are gold, and Shee;
>   Us she inform'd, but transubstantiates you;

> Soft dispositions which ductile bee,
> Elixarlike, she makes not cleane, but new; [51]

and in "The First Anniversary" he describes Elizabeth Drury as one

> Who, though she could not transubstantiate
> All states to gold, yet guilded every state.[52]

In the seesaw of hyperbolic praise and scurrilous criticism which is Elegie VIII, "The Comparison," he asserts that the cherishing heat of his mistress' "best-lov'd part" is like

> the Chymicks masculine equall fire,
> Which in the Lymbecks warme wombe doth
> inspire
> Into th'earths worthlesse durt a soule of gold.[53]

It is an interesting fact that little of the cynicism of what was probably his actual opinion of alchemy creeps into Donne's imagery. It does so, and richly—in a poem which is itself called "Loves Alchymie"—when, discoursing on that favorite theme, the lover's illusion of happiness, he says:

> Oh, 'tis imposture all:
> And as no chymique yet th'Elixir got,
> But glorifies his pregnant pot,
> If by the way to him befall
> Some odoriferous thing, or medicinall,
> So, lovers dreame a rich and long delight,
> But get a winter-seeming summers night; [54]

and, even more directly, when he says in "The Crosse":

> as oft Alchimists doe coyners prove,
> So may a selfe-dispising, get selfe-love.[55]

Despite these it is evident that, given the free rein which is imagery, Donne's imagination preferred to explore the exotic and mysterious deeds alchemy might perform than the quackery which really accompanied it.

A word may be added here concerning a few images from other practices typical of the Elizabethan alchemist. From the secret books of the dabblers in the black arts comes the comparison between poorly made coins and the

> many angled figures, in the booke
> Of some great Conjurer; [56]

and the specular stone—probably the magic mirror or show stone used by Dr. Dee *—is the source of the image when he says, in the course of a eulogy of Lady Bedford,

> You teach (though wee learne not) a thing
> unknowne
> To our late times, the use of specular stone,
> Through which all things within without
> were shown;[57]

and again when he observes that it is futile to tell men to love virtuous women, when there are no more—just as it would be

> but madnes now t'impart
> The skill of specular stone,
> When he which can have learn'd the art
> To cut it, can finde none.[58]

Although occasionally carried away by their own virtuosity, these images from medicine and alchemy bring to bear the sharply focussed light of technical procedures and terminology on the haze that surrounds the expression of states of feeling and spiritual attitudes. In so far as they tend toward the precise, the complex, and the unexploited, such figures strengthen the tentative observation made at the close of the preceding chapter.

---

* E. K. Chambers, editor, *Poems of John Donne,* New York, Scribners, 1901, I, 222-223.

V

GEOMETRY AND THE CIRCLE

Throughout Donne's writings there occur, like a series of bright strange lights, images utilizing the idea of a circle. Even the casual reader becomes aware of their frequency; while to one who studies the entire body of his poetry and prose this recurrence assumes the proportions of a series of elaborate variations on a theme. The theme is perfection, completeness, infinity—and the circle is its symbol; this Donne makes clear in image after image. In fact, its relation to these allied conceptions is so consistent as to form one of the most vivid and distinctive of the associations in his imagery.

The attribution of mystic properties to numbers and geometric figures is probably as old as mathematics itself. More than five centuries before Christ, Pythagoras developed a veritable philosophy of occult correspondencies between numbers and ideas. We need not go beyond Donne himself to illustrate the influence of this tradition: in the *Essays in Divinity,* speaking of the laws of Scripture, he wrote: "It hath also three hundred and sixty-five negative precepts; and so many sinews and ligatures hath our body, and so many days the year"; [1] and on several occasions, referring to an esoteric attribute of one of the most mystic of numbers,[*] he declared, "Seven is infinite." [2] In "The Primrose" it is five that proves mysterious; the flower has five petals, he observes, and let

---

[*] David Eugene Smith, *History of Mathematics,* New York, Ginn and Co., 1923-1925, II, 2.

> women, whom this flower doth represent,
> With this mysterious number be content.[3]

It recalls Sir Thomas Browne's "The Garden of Cyrus"—strange dissertation on the mysteries of the quincunx.

But it is the circle image which attracts Donne like a magnet. Anticipations of his speculations on it can be found in many places. Thus Aristotle, blending mathematics with a little mysticism, wrote: ". . . there is nothing strange in the circle being the origin of any and every marvel," and pointed out that it is made up of contraries, that it is both concave and convex, moves in two directions at once, and comes back to the place from which it starts.[*] In the very edition of Euclid from which Donne probably drew most of his knowledge of geometry there is added to the otherwise unadorned definition of the circle the *obiter dictum* that "of all figures a circle is the most perfect." [†] The idea of the circle's perfection and infinity naturally suggests an identification with the deity. And so we find St. Bonaventura describing God as "a circle whose centre is everywhere, whose circumference nowhere." [**]

The circle may have had semi-mystical ideas associated with it many times in its history, but in Donne it was to undergo, surely as never before, the most fanciful exploration and the strangest of its sea-changes into poetry and prose. Occasionally all of nature becomes, in Donne's eyes, a veritable vision of circles. God, he declares in a direct observation, has made all things in a roundness—"from the round superficies of this earth . . . to the round convexity of those heavens . . . God hath wrapped up all

---

[*] "Mechanica," tr. E. E. Foster in *The Works of Aristotle,* Oxford, 1913, VI, 847b-848a.

[†] *The Elements of Geometrie . . . of Euclide of Megara,* tr. H. Billingsley. Imprinted at London by John Daye, 1570, Definition 15.

[**] Quoted by *Grierson,* II, 176.

things in circles." It is the signature, the emblem, "one of the most convenient hieroglyphics" of God, Donne says in a sermon, for He, too, is endless, that is, "whom God loves, he loves to the end." [4] Moreover, he adds elsewhere that although He is so much a circle as to be everywhere without corner, that is, "never hid from our inquisition," yet he is nowhere a straight line, that is, able to be "directly and presently beheld and contemplated." [5] Only in his working on us, he says in his *Devotions,* is God a direct line.[6]

If God is a circle, what is more logical than that any impossible suggestion concerning him should be denoted by that oldest of mathematical puzzles—squaring the circle. If, for example, we agree that the best epithet for Him is "Eternal God," then

> who ever dare
> Seeke new expressions, doe the Circle square,
> And thrust into strait corners of poore wit
> Thee, who art cornerlesse and infinite.[7]

Men, Donne observes in a prose passage, who seek to find in themselves doubt of the infiniteness of God's mercy are also trying to square the circle, for their attempts are not only unnatural, but would, if successful, give to the circle those ominous angles and corners mentioned above.[8]

Several images involve diameters. In one he points out that just as each diameter must pass through the center, flow from the center, and look to it from above or below, so each man's acts must pass through God and be to his glory, whether in the sight of men below or God above, whether in this life or the next.[9] Typical of the fantastic festoonery of "The Second Anniversary" is the exhortation to the soul that, like a diameter which touches the center once and the circumference twice, it should

spend twice as much thought on heaven as it had concerning earth.[10] Lastly, there is the picture of the time
from Christ's first coming to his second as a circle of
which no man knows the diameter.[11]

Closely related to these, but presented, as is Donne's
habit in verse, with all the flesh of explanation and con-
nective cut away, is the description of just how religious
feeling permeates the truly religious and radiates from
them:

> In those poor types of God (round circles) so
> Religious tipes, the peecelesse centers flow,
> And are in all the lines which all wayes goe.[12]

Meditations upon God, declares Donne, surely referring
to just such meditations as these, are infinite—and therefore they themselves suggest the circle figure, for whatever is infinite is "circular, and returns into itself, and is
everywhere beginning and ending, and yet nowhere
either. . . ."[13]

The next major concept caught in the web of this
imagery of lines and circles is the life of man—his progress from birth to death. This life is also a circle, one
that is in every case completed perfectly, for, in the classic
epitome of the Bible, "Dust thou art, and to dust thou
must return."[14] Since, of all forms, "a circle is the per-
fectest . . . art thou loath," Donne asks, "to make up that
circle, with returning to the earth again?"[15] Consider
yourself, he admonishes elsewhere, and you will see how
the two ends of the circle meet, how you go "from one
mother to another, from the wombe to the grave."[16] The
day of death is merely the last piece to a circle; in contrast,
the Day of Judgment is an everlasting one that knows
no pieces.[17]

The circle, to be drawn unerringly, involves the geometer's compass; and this opens up to Donne another little world of curious metaphor. The instrument image, added to the circle image, produces in every case a figure of extraordinary precision and challenging—not to say inordinate—complexity. Sometimes the parallel is pursued through such thickets of symbolism that if the reader but lift his eyes the trail is lost. Such is the following, wherein Donne, his illness abating, illustrates why he must continue to put all faith in God if he is to expect further results from the treatment of physicians:

> As hee that would describe a circle in paper, if hee
> have brought that circle within one inch of finish-
> ing, yet if he remove his compasse, he cannot make
> it up a perfit circle, except he fall to worke again,
> to finde out the same center, so, though setting that
> foot of my compasse upon thee, I have gone so
> farre, as to the consideration of my selfe, yet if I
> depart from thee, my center, all is unperfit.[18]

In this instance the effect is further blunted by the confusing sentence structure and punctuation, a not unusual weakness of Elizabethan-Jacobean prose. In the "Obsequies to the Lord Harrington" we get a circle image and a compass image so involved that they appear to be mixed:

> O soule, O circle, why so quickly bee
> Thy ends, thy birth and death, clos'd up in thee?
> Since one foot of thy compasse still was plac'd
> In heav'n, the other might securely'have pac'd
> In the most large extent, through every path,
> Which the whole world, or man the
>   abridgment hath.[19]

It is apparent that the two images are not really mixed, but that each independently—the circle in the first couplet and the compass in the remaining lines—expresses Donne's regret over the short life of the dead nobleman.

In at least two other passages Donne sees the figure of the compass circle in the lives of men. In one he points out that the body of man was "the first point that the foot of God's compass" touched and that He then moved the compass around and ended where he began—with the body of man in resurrection.[20] In another he says that, in the case of a martyr, death ends one circle only to begin another—for the eternity of immortality is a circle, too. However, where this life is a circle made with a compass that passes from point to point, that immortal life after death is a circle

> stamped with a print, an endless, and perfect circle, as soon as it begins. Of this circle, the mathematician is . . . God; the other circle we make up ourselves. . . .[21]

It is a striking distinction; and so effective seemed the image of the circle printed all at once that Donne used it a second time—to illustrate the way in which the beginning of God's love insures, and thus contains, love to the end.[22]

The last of these compass-circle figures, but probably the most famous, and at one time perhaps the most notorious of "metaphysical" images, is that which runs through the last twelve lines of "A Valediction: forbidding mourning." The poet, about to leave for the continent, enters another in a remarkable series of denials that a parting between true lovers is a parting. If our two souls are two, he says,

> they are two so
> As stiffe twin compasses are two,

> Thy soule the fixt foot, makes no show
>   To move, but doth, if the'other doe.
>
> And though it in the center sit,
>   Yet when the other far doth rome,
> It leanes, and hearkens after it,
>   And growes erect, as that comes home.
>
> Such wilt thou be to mee, who must
>   Like th'other foot, obliquely runne;
> Thy firmnes makes my circle just,
>   And makes me end, where I begunne.[23]

Here Donne brings to bear the precision and concreteness of a mathematical instrument in dealing with one of the most nebulous of spiritual relationships; and part of the triumph of the image lies in its success in clarifying that relationship without materializing its spiritual essence. The sources of its effectiveness as an image are manifold: there is the unexpectedness in such a connection of the entire analogy, the surprise at each of the successive subordinate parallels, the logic of their sequence, and the utilization in the close of the finality of a circle completed and the inherently satisfactory idea of perfect completion coinciding with perfect completion.

A few other figures deserve passing attention. When Donne involves the circle in his praise of Elizabeth Drury, we can expect extravagance. The very completeness of her perfections suggests the circle to him.[24] In another place he goes even further: If we compare her proportions to cubes, he says, they are unstable; if to circles, they are angular.[25] In other words, compared to Elizabeth Drury, the paragons of proportion are sadly disproportionate. Even if it were true, as Drummond of Hawthornden reported, that Donne told Ben Jonson that the "Anniversaries" described "the Idea of Woman, and not as she was," he still overreached himself in such imagery.

But the most extravagant of all is the circle figure running through the "Elegie upon Prince Henry." Donne is said to have declared that he wrote the poem "to match Sir Edward Herbert in obscurenesse." He seems to have succeeded. In it he describes reason as the center of a circle embracing the entire natural world, and faith as the center of one that embraces such ideas as God's essence and the where, when, and how of souls. Reason, if sufficiently extended, almost meets faith, and thus almost makes the two circles concentric. This, Donne says, came nearest to happening in the case of the dead prince,

> For all that faith might credit mankinde could,
> Reason still seconded, that this prince would.[26]

Coldness or lack of feeling may perhaps occasionally be overlooked, but a figure so strained and tortuous seems beyond excuse; it was such images that caused certain eighteenth century critics to think of Donne's verse only as an example of bad taste.

A mathematical point, Donne observes in one of his letters, is "the most indivisible and unique thing which art can present." Most indivisible and unique, it is for Donne a fitting image of man's soul, and, once again, of God.[27] Similarly, the virtue of a man like Lord Harrington is best described not as of "the purest parts," but as without parts, just simple,

> for a point and one
> Are much entirer than a million.[28]

Again, referring to an elementary distinction between points and lines, he speaks of the uncertainty and incoherence of life at court as "a line discontinued, and a number of small wretched points, uselesse, because they concurre not"; [29] and he embarks entirely upon the technical terminology of the geometer when he declares that it was impossible to find any one dominant element or humour in Elizabeth Drury's character, for,

> though all doe know, that quantities
> Are made of lines, and lines from Points arise,
> None can these lines or quantities unjoynt,
> And say this is a line, or this a point.[30]

For a student to speculate on such esoteric relationships between points and lines would not be remarkable, but for the poet to utilize them is another thing. Donne alone of the poets of his time—perhaps of any time except the present—would have ventured to use such materials so thoroughly and uncompromisingly. Obviously he was not always successful; but the significant thing here is that as a source of imagery this entire branch of learning, so fertile for Donne was virtually barren for his contemporaries.

It is apparent, too, that of all the sources we are likely to deal with geometry represents an apex in the logic and precision of its statements and the finality of its definitions —particularly with reference to the most complex and subtle relationships. Its symbols and propositions are, in fact, as purely intellectual as any that science offers. Consequently, when applied as Donne applies them—to the clarification or heightening of his conceptions of God, religion, the soul, immortality or love, the effect of these images is a crystallization of such ethical and spiritual themes with their vague emotional overtones into clearly delineated, adequately complex, and peculiarly objective terms. This is part of that intellectual transubstantiation of emotion which lies at the core of the effect of Donne's

work; at its peak, as in the compass image of "A Valediction: forbidding mourning," the poet comes as near a
satifactory intellectual statement of the dimensions and
nature of particular emotions as poetry has known.

VI

LAW COURTS AND PRISONS

The knowledge of law and courts of law that a literary work may reveal usually comes to an author through contacts of the type that almost any individual inevitably has with both. A writer who is—like Bacon or Sir John Davies, for example—a lifelong practitioner in all the branches of the profession and initiate in all its mysteries is surely the exception. It is interesting to note, then, that Donne, from the point of view of biography, is much closer to the latter. After leaving Cambridge he registered at Lincoln's Inn, one of the four great Elizabethan Inns of Court for lawyers and students. Although he did not continue there long, he apparently remained interested in the society, for, soon after he took orders in 1615, he was chosen Reader in Divinity to the Benchers of the Inn and held that title from 1616 to 1622. Moreover, Gosse points out that even just before he was ordained it was rumored, while he was still travelling in France, that he was going to take the degree of Doctor of Laws. To put an end to this tale he wrote to a friend in England: *

> For my purpose of proceeding in the profession of the law, so farre as to a title you may be pleased to correct that imagination, wheresoever you finde it;

but just as interesting is the observation he adds immediately:

---

* Edmund Gosse, *The Life and Letters of John Donne,* London, Dodd, Mead, 1899, I, 303; hereafter designated as *Gosse.*

I ever thought the study of it my best entertain-
tainment, and pastime, but I have no ambition, nor
designe upon the style.[1]

All this would seem to indicate a strong interest in the
law and a semi-professional attitude toward it; this, however, is only imperfectly reflected in his imagery. A few
images draw upon what may be considered professional
knowledge; the remainder — and their number is not
great—are interesting and characteristic in style but seem
to me to be based upon information which any observant
layman might acquire. If there appears to be something
of a disparity here, we have a passage in Satyre II which,
although it is not without echoes of classical models and
traditions, might well help to explain it. He is describing
Coscus, a lawyer so full of his profession that he cannot
speak a syllable without letting the world know what his
work is. Such is his state, says Donne, that

> he throwes
> Like nets, or lime-twigs, wheresoever he goes,
> His title of Barrister, on every wench,
> And wooes in language of the Pleas, and Bench:
> A motion, Lady; Speake Coscus; I have beene
> In love, ever since *tricesimo* of the Queene,
> Continuall claims I have made, injunctions got
> To stay my rivals suit, that hee should not
> Proceed; spare mee; In Hillary terme I went,
> You said, If I return'd next size in Lent,
> I should be in remitter of your grace;
> In th'interim my letters should take place
> Of affidavits.[2]

Lest anyone remain in doubt as to just what his opinion
of such jargon is, Donne adds:

> words, words, which would teare
> The tender labyrinth of a soft maids eare.

But even as he ridicules such a penchant for legal phraseology—a penchant which, in fact, had been popular in the Elizabethan sonnet tradition — he shows the technical grasp we might have expected. *Tricesimo,* Hilary term and Lent assizes, the making of motions in court, and injunctions got to stay a rival, are handled familiarly if to absurd effect.

Somewhat more esoteric than these are the figures he uses when he describes God's giving way in a small matter as not a cancelling of patent but only a *supersedeas* not to execute it at that time;[3] and Love—who has grown so great that he can even hold sway in the heart of the Earl of Somerset—as

> Our little Cupid hath sued Livery,
> And is no more in his minority,[4]

a reference to the ancient procedure whereby a ward, arriving at majority, sued his guardian for delivery of his property. In "Loves Exchange," resigned to the fact that he has given his soul to love and received nothing in return, he says to the God of Love:

> I do not sue from thee to draw
> A *non obstante* * on natures law,
> These are prerogatives, they inhere
> In thee and thine;[5]

in "Loves Diet," receiving a favorable letter from one whom he has pursued, he checks his impulse to love by asking cynically:

---

* An act of the king by which a law was dispensed with and its violation authorized.

> if any title bee
> Convey'd by this, Ah, what doth it availe,
> To be the fortieth name in an entaile? [6]

and in "A Valediction: of the booke" he remarks of the
letters which have passed between him and his lover:

> Here more then in their bookes may Lawyers
>   finde,
> Both by what titles Mistresses are ours,
> And how prerogative these states devours,
> Transferr'd from Love himselfe, to womankinde. [7]

In such imagery we once again get aspects of God and
Love, each essentially a thing of the spirit, illustrated by
means of the most prosaic—and precise—of worldly parallels. Elsewhere we find images based on the taking of evidence, arraignment, bribery by letter or fee, the possession
of legal title, and the trying of principals before acces-
sories; and this represents the extent of what may be
deemed Donne's special knowledge of the law.

Equally related to the legal profession, but based as
much on observation of human nature as on an interest in
technical niceties, are those images whose source is the
actions of men, both officers of law and criminals, in the
routine of court and prison. The poor lawyer—of the
Coscus variety, one supposes—must at one moment run
around with bills, at another stand and talk idly,

> like prisoners, which whole months will
>   sweare
> That onely suretiship hath brought them there, [8]

and at a third,

> more shamelesse farre
> Then carted whores, lye, to the grave Judge. . . . [9]

Thus, adding insult to injury, he describes the work of the
lawyers as sordid, and does so in imagery drawn from the

characteristics of common prisoners.

A scene probably as familiar as these is the one utilized when a young gallant suggests to his inamorata how he may be catechized if he is caught by her father:

> Once, and but once found in thy company,
> All thy suppos'd escapes are laid on mee;
> And as a thiefe at barre, is question'd there
> By all the men, that have beene rob'd that yeare,
> So am I; [10]

and a contemptuous comment on playwrights is made absolutely withering by a courtroom simile. Such a hack

> (like a wretch, which at Barre judg'd as dead,
> Yet prompts him which stands next, and cannot
> reade,
> And saves his life) gives ideot actors meanes
> (Starving himselfe) to live by his labor'd sceanes. [11]

This is a strikingly vivid use of the fantastic custom of allowing defendants who could read to plead "benefit of clergy" and thus go free. Another figure supplied by a similar courtroom tableau occurs when he says of the silence of those stricken by grief,

> So guiltiest men stand mutest at the barre; [12]

but here the accuracy of the interpretation is perhaps questionable.

Judging from the frequency of its appearance in his imagery a prison cell is to Donne the perfect symbol of man bereft of will and freedom of spirit. Such an attitude is usually conventional but in Donne's case it may well have gone back to a very unpleasant personal experience: in 1602 Sir George More, enraged by his daughter's clandestine marriage to Donne, had had the young man

thrown into "the Fleet" for violating the Canon Law. He
was there only a few days but long enough to leave us
several letters postmarked from the famous prison.*
Among these images we find first the ever-recurring,
basically religious conception of the body as a prison.
Made of base stuff, it drags down the noble soul. Flesh,
he declares on several occasions, is the clay in which this
prison of the soul is built.[13] Elaborating this idea, he wrote
to Lady Bedford:

> As men to'our prisons, new soules to us are sent,
> Which learne vice there, and come in innocent.[14]

Fevers and the vapor sickness are respectively a burning
and a blowing down of the prison.[15] Death is delivery.[16]
It is the gate out of the prison, he adds elsewhere; and
thus a gentle sickness leading up to death is an oiled key
to the gate, while violent death is a sudden hewing down
of it.[17]

Illness, which is the corrupting of this body, also takes
man's liberty from him and crushes his spirit, and therefore anything connected with that is a prison. His sickbed
is such a place [18]—and one that affords him not even the
usual prison-cell minimum of two or three steps of liberty.[19] ". . . when I am cast into this bedd," he cries out
in his *Devotions*, "my slacke sinewes are yron fetters, and
those thin sheets, yron dores upon me. . . ." [20] At such a
time, as one of his letters declares, even his house becomes
a dungeon.[21] Probably unconscious of how logically he
was developing this deep-rooted association he wrote to
Sir Robert Karre:

> Though I have left my bed, I have not left my bed-
> side; I sit there still, and as a Prisoner discharged

---

* See *Gosse*, I, 103–106.

sits at the Prison doore, to beg Fees, so sit I here, to gather crummes.[22]

Reference is made here to the vicious system whereby prisoners, who had to pay fees to the jailer, might be kept in jail until such payment was forthcoming.* Apparently they were sometimes reduced to begging at the prison door. In any case, Donne used the image effectively on several occasions—once to figure the situation of a fleet becalmed in the harbor, and, at another time, that of a babe bound to the womb by a cord even after birth.[23]

Because a great number of crimes were punishable by death and many suffered such punishment, the machinery of execution was everywhere visible. Such all too vivid circumstances furnish the background when Donne exclaims:

> . . . in our mothers' wombs, we are close prisoners all; when we are born, we are born but to the liberty of the house; prisoners still, though within larger walls: and then all our life is but a going out to the place of execution, to death. Now was there ever any man seen to sleep in the cart, between Newgate, and Tyburn? between the prison, and the place of execution, does any man sleep? And we sleep all the way; from the womb to the grave we are never thoroughly awake. . . .[24]

It is estimated, moreover, that every year almost a thousand persons rode to the gallows in Elizabeth's England. Usually the gallows-tree stood at the edge of the city; and even in this Donne finds substance for an analogy. He who realizes that after death the Holy City is not far off is like one who, travelling "weary, and late towards a great city,

---

* See *Grierson*, II, 135–136.

is glad when he comes to a place of execution, because he knows that is near the town." [25] In addition, hanging, drawing, and quartering was still the usual punishment for treason, and so, describing—in the slanderous mood of Elegie VIII—another's despised mistress, he writes:

> Like Sun-parch'd quarters on the citie gate,
> Such is thy tann'd skins lamentable state.[26]

Drawing and quartering was not the worst of the barbarisms practiced—even the rack was still used occasionally. In its torture Donne finds a figure for love, on the one hand, and, on the other, for the condition that comes of the lack of His word.[27]

Finally we get at least three vivid pictures from the ways of thieves. In one, the soul at the final summons is described as

> a thiefe, which till deaths doome be read,
> Wisheth himselfe delivered from prison;
> But damn'd and hal'd to execution,
> Wisheth that still he might be imprisoned,[28]

and, in the second, a writer who miscited when his opponents were watching most carefully reminds him of a thief who leaves a covert to meet a strong hue and cry in the teeth.[29] In the third, an old and familiar way of trailing men supplies a clear and subtly conceived image when Sapho is made to say that she left no more sign of her dalliance with Philaenis than birds leave in air, while

> Men leave behinde them that which their sin
>   showes,
> And are as theeves trac'd, which rob when
>   it snows.[30]

Although the small group of technical and esoteric images which we reviewed in the opening part of this chapter fits in with the pattern of tendencies outlined in earlier chapters, it is evident that figures making extensive or intensive use of legal concepts and forms play no great part in Donne. Despite the fact that he was apparently much interested in law and that its more recondite and intricate aspects might often have served his purposes, it seems evident that his aversion to using what had already been overworked—and by men writing in a tradition against which he rebelled—was enough to curb sharply his tendency toward such imagery.

VII

RELIGION AND THE BIBLE

A study of direct references or allusions in Donne's works would yield such an overwhelming number and variety related to religion that all other references would seem unimportant by comparison. This is obviously because references are an integral part of subject matter and the subject matter of almost all of Donne's prose and a fourth or fifth part of his poetry is religious devotion or theological exegesis. But imagery has, as we have seen, no such restricted relation to subject matter; as soon as we begin to examine Donne's images we find that those from religion not only do not show a corresponding preponderance but actually occur no more often than the images from half a dozen other sources and not so effectively or analytically as those from two or three we have already considered.

There are, however, two circumstances which suggest at least a partial explanation of this situation: at the time of his early writings Donne's all-engrossing interest in religion had not yet manifested itself, and in his later works the very fact that their subject matter was religion made it only natural that he should avoid religious imagery— only natural, I say, because Donne's imagery makes clear that he accepted fully the conception of an image as an illumination of one idea by another not related to it in subject matter. In the early period he had no very great imaginative interest in religion, and, in the latter, what appears to be an elementary dictate of style prevented him from giving expression to it by way of imagery.

Outside of this, perhaps the most interesting fact concerning Donne's images from religion is that the majority of them are used to illuminate not things of the spirit or the worship of God but the profane love of woman and the extravagant praise of patrons. In his lyrics, "elegies," and marriage songs he develops a veritable religion of love, and in his letters—both in verse and in prose—obsequies, and "Anniversaries," a parallel religion of patronage. One of the basic propositions of the first of these is that love is a holy mystery in which only the lovers are initiates. In fact, it would be, the poet avers,

> prophanation of our joyes
> To tell the layetie our love.[1]

The annals of our relationship, he boasts to one mistress, will act as Scriptures for lovers of posterity:

> There, the faith of any ground
> No schismatique will dare to wound,

and therein

> . . . Loves Divines, (since all Divinity
> Is love or wonder) may finde all they seeke.[2]

In another lyric which he actually calls "The Canonization" his love verses become part of the ceremony of sanctification in the church of love:

> And by these hymnes, all shall approve
> Us Canoniz'd for Love.[3]

He who has suffered from "loves hot fires," he explains, becomes a martyr,[4] and anything connected with him or his love has something of the sacred about it. Thus in "The Funerall" he says of a wreath of hair, memento of a lost love, which he wears on his arm:

> bury it with me,
> For since I am
> Loves martyr, it might breed idolatrie,
> If into others hands these Reliques came; [5]

and in Elegie XII, when circumstances force him from his mistress, he becomes a holy man put to torture. "Is't because thou thy self art blind," he importunes the God of Love, "that wee

> Thy Martyrs must no more each other see?
> Or tak'st thou pride to break us on the wheel
>
> . . .
>
> Or have we left undone some mutual Right,
> Through holy fear, that merits thy despight? [6]

Attitudes which are in any way rebellious suggest either of the two major types of religious revolt, heresy or atheism. In the cynical mood of the "Farewell to Love" he asserts:

> Whilst yet to prove,
> I thought there was some Deitie in love
> So did I reverence, and gave
> Worship; as Atheists at their dying houre
> Call, what they cannot name, an unknowne
> power; [7]

while in the arrant perversity and paganism of "The Indifferent" he pretends that promiscuity is orthodox and fidelity the reverse:

> . . . Some two or three
> Poore Heretiques in love there bee,
> Which thinke to stablish dangerous constancie. [8]

In "Loves Deitie," finding himself rebellious under the tyrannical edict of the God of Love whereby he is fated to love one who does not love him, he berates himself:

> Rebell and Atheist too, why murmure I,
> As though I felt the worst that love could
> doe? [9]

and in Elegie VI he compares a lover's revolt with the greatest of schisms within the Christian church:

> . . . I shall
> As nations do from Rome, from thy love fall

and

> when I
> Am the Recusant, in that resolute state,
> What hurts it mee to be'excommunicate? [10]

Donne finds parallels for all the rites of love and marriage, even to the most private, in church ceremony. Thus in one place the bridal bed is "loves hallow'd temple" and in another it is love's altar on which the bride is a pleasing sacrifice.[11] In embrace, the lovers are as nice as "Priests in handling reverent sacrifice"; [12] and in the "Epithalamion made at Lincolnes Inne" the bride

> at the Bridegroomes wish'd approach doth lye,
> Like an appointed lambe, when tenderly
> The priest comes on his knees t'embowell her.[13]

Of the minor figures in this group we may mention that in which vows and acts of love are described as faith and good works, a lapse from love as apostasy, a fickle mistress as purgatory, and the home of a mistress' husband as his diocese.[14]

This fusion of the holy and the erotic is made even more conspicuous by a few images wherein the terms are completely reversed and religious devotion becomes a sexual relationship. It is worth noting, too, that these few figures are virtually the only ones drawn from the love relationship. In Holy Sonnet XIX he refers to the "flatter-

ing speaches" with which he "courts" God;[15] and in Holy
Sonnet XVIII, speaking of the Church of God, he says:

> . . . let myne amorous soule court thy mild
>   Dove,
> Who is most trew, and pleasing to thee, then
> When she'is embrac'd and open to most men.[16]

The approach to God as a kind of holy mistress is evident
throughout the second half of "A Hymne to Christ"; in
the last stanza he declares:

> Seale then this bill of my Divorce to All,
> On whom those fainter beames of love did fall;
> Marry those loves, which in youth scattered bee
> On Fame, Wit, Hopes (false mistresses) to thee.[17]

But probably the most passionate of these is the plea addressed to God in Holy Sonnet XIV:

> Yet dearely'I love you, 'and would be loved faine,
> But am betroth'd unto your enemie:
> Divorce mee, 'untie, or breake that knot againe,
> Take mee to you, imprison mee, for I
> . . . . never shall be free,
> Nor ever chast, except you ravish mee.[18]

It was perhaps of such figures that Saintsbury was thinking when he said of Donne that in his later age he did but
"trans-hallow his profanities." At least once Donne himself referred openly to this transference; in Holy Sonnet
XIII he tells his soul that he addresses her with just such
words

>   as in my idolatrie
> I said to all my profane mistresses.[19]

*   *

Donne's tendency to address patrons in images which
suggest that they are deities and that the praise bestowed

on them is part of a holy ritual can hardly be considered an unwitting or even ingenuous revelation of feeling. It was part of an established tradition of patron worship wherein the worshipers propitiated their Gods and Goddesses with wreaths of conceits and an incense of extravagant flattery. Far from being loathe to disclose his function as high-priest, Donne makes much of it. To the Countess of Huntingdon he writes:

> I was your Prophet in your yonger dayes,
> And now your Chaplaine, God in you to praise; [20]

and, adopting completely the nomenclature of the church and its hierarchies, he writes to Lady Carey and Mrs. Essex Riche:

> Yet turning to Saincts, should my'humility
> To other Sainct then you directed bee,
> That were to make my schisme, heresie.
>
> Nor would I be a Convertite so cold,
> As not to tell it;

and

> I thought it some Apostleship in mee
> To speake things which by faith alone I see. [21]

It is Lady Bedford—patron of so many of the great writers of the time that one could almost believe the outpourings of eulogy with which they deluged her—that Donne addressed most often in such terms. One of the most elaborate and artificial of these figures is that in which he describes her soul as a deity dwelling in the temple of her body:

> Yet to that Deity which dwels in you,
> Your vertuous Soule, I now not sacrifice;
> These are Petitions, and not Hymnes; they sue

But that I may survay the edifice.

> In all Religions as much care hath bin
> Of Temples frames, and beauty, 'as Rites
> within.

> As all which goe to Rome, doe not thereby
> Esteeme religions. . . .

so

> in this pilgrimage I would behold
> You as you'are vertues temple . . .

and,

> oppose to all
> Bablers of chappels, you th'Escuriall.[22]

In much the same vein he wrote to her that

> Reason is our Soules left hand, Faith her right,
> By these wee reach divinity, that's you;

that, moreover, her virtues were so infinitely beyond reason's reach that he must fall back on faith,

> And rest on what the Catholique voice doth teach;

> That you are good: and not one Heretique
> Denies it. . . .[23]

He obviously believes that no self-abasement before such a deity is excessive; she will not scorn his praises, he says, for as

> In labourers balads oft more piety
> God findes, then in *Te Deums* melodie.[24]

Donne knew of course that all this was the most immoderate kind of flattery—knew it so well that he took cognizance of it, perhaps hoping thereby to mitigate its artificiality. Referring to a number of fantastic and strained conceits which he has just lavished on her, he says to Lady Bedford:

> But these (as nice thinne Schoole divinity
> Serves heresie to furder or represse)

> Tast of Poëtique rage, or flattery,
> And need not, where all hearts one truth
>   professe.[25]

Knowing, too, that such paeans of praise were hardly the most pious use to which sacred ideas might be put, he seeks to fortify his procedure with an ingenious parallel from the practice of the early Christians:

> Temples were not demolish'd, though prophane:
>   Here Peter Joves, there Paul hath Dian's Fane.
> So whether my hymnes you admit or chuse,
>   In me you'have hallowed a Pagan Muse.[26]

Even the explanation that Donne offered for his excessive adoration of Elizabeth Drury—that it was the Idea of woman he was thinking of—hardly serves to make palatable such application of the supposedly sacred to such a distinctly secular relationship.

Of the religious images which Donne used to illuminate his attitudes towards other things besides mistresses and patrons few demand particular attention. All in all they form a miscellany of passing allusions to common aspects of religious theory and church practice—to God, the Saviour, and Satan; hell, heaven, and angels; temple, cloister, monastery, diocese, and pew; nun, vicar, chorister, and parishioner; chalice and prayer; schismatic, heretic, and anchorite. Moreover, it is not difficult to find further evidence here of the same somewhat irreverent tendency to apply religious images to arrantly profane ideas. Thus in Satyre IIII, for example, he describes a fatuous courtier as stopping to preen in order to

> call his clothes to shrift,
> Making them confesse not only mortall
> Great staines and holes in them; but veniall
> Feathers and dust, wherewith they fornicate,

and entering a room a moment later

> with such nicetie
> As a young Preacher at his first time goes
> To preach.[27]

If such a tendency does seem unregenerate, it is only just
to point out that these images, as well as those applied
to his mistresses and patrons, appear in his very early
lyrics and satires and in verse letters written before he
took orders.

It is a significant, not to say astonishing fact that
there are in this group virtually no images from the complex abstractions and recondite speculation which characterize the writings of the older theologians in general and
the Scholastic thinkers in particulars. The nearest Donne
comes to these is when he uses the idea of free will in a
letter to Sir Robert Karre:

> If my Muse were onely out of fashion, and but
> wounded and maimed like Free-will in the Roman
> Church, I should adventure to put her to an Epi-
> thalamion. But since she is dead, like Free-will in
> our Church, I have not so much Muse left as to
> lament her losse,[28]

or the mystic trinity in a verse tribute to a friend:

> . . . that mistique trinitee
> Whereof thou'and all to whom heavens do infuse
> Like fyer, are made; thy body, mind, and Muse;[29]

and there is little enough of the abstract or speculative
about these.

Even religion yields bizarre figures to Donne's imagination; here as elsewhere the most unusual phases of the
source subject are made to serve his purpose. Think, he
says,

> that no stubborne sullen Anchorit,
> Which fixt to a pillar, or a grave, doth sit
> Bedded, and bath'd in all his ordures, dwels
> So fowly as our Soules in their first-built Cels; [30]

and again, to illustrate how much of a prison a sickbed is, he observes that even the "Anchorites that barqu'd themselves up in hollowe trees, and immur'd themselves in hollow walls . . . could stand, or sit," and were free by comparison.[31]

We may close this section with two of the very few images which he derives from the great religious controversy of his time. In Satyrs I, by way of general disparagement he addresses a typical coxcomb as

> Oh monstrous, superstitious puritan,[32]

while in Satyre II, as if to balance the record without delay, he derides certain poetasters as

> poore, disarm'd, like Papists, not worth hate.[33]

It is interesting to note Donne's use of these extremist positions in religion simply as symbols of the contemptible.

BIBLE STORY

When we remember that the incidents and characters of the Bible were as familiar to the average Elizabethan, and particularly to one who was a clergyman, as those in his own life, the images Donne draws from Scripture appear to be neither numerous nor unusual. The stories he utilizes are, in fact, among the most popular. From the Old Testament, which yields by far the greater number, comes, first, the description of Creation. Admitting to the Countess of Salisbury that he has praised others as he praises her now, he nevertheless denies that he is in any way belying himself. If God had made man before anything else, he observes,

> and man had seene
> The third daies fruits, and flowers, and various
>   greene,
> He might have said the best that he could say
> Of those faire creatures, which were made that
>   day;
> And when next day he had admir'd the birth
> Of Sun, Moone, Stars, fairer then late-prais'd
>   earth,
> Hee might have said the best that he could say—[34]

and no more belie himself than did Donne.

The idea of Paradise itself Donne uses again and again, usually to signify, conventionally enough, perfect circumstances or a state of bliss. From this source comes the popular conception of the serpent and the tale of the cursing of Cain. The serpent, because it is slippery yet entangling, symbolizes the idea of the Trinity; [35] while of one who betrayed him and his love he says:

> Curst may hee be, that so our love hath slaine,
>   And wander on the earth, wretched as Cain.[36]

He uses, besides these, the story of Noah and the beasts of the Ark, Sara's joy at finding that she is with child, the account of Nebuchadnezzar foraging in the field, Samson's unhappy fate—

> Like slacke sinew'd Sampson, his haire off,
> Languish our ships,[37]

and the tower of Babel—

> They who did labour Babels tower to'erect,
> Might have considered, that for that effect,
> All this whole solid Earth could not allow
> Nor furnish forth materialls enow,

just as

> No more affords this world, foundation
> To erect true joy. . . .[38]

The miracle of those who were cast into the furnace and
came forth unharmed occurs to him several times—as
when he says that those sailors who manage to survive
equatorial heat

> that miracle do multiply
> Where walkers in hot Ovens, doe not dye.[39]

But it is the accounts of Moses, the burning bush, and the
Exodus, which seem to prove most attractive. Describing
Lady Marckham he wrote:

> Her heart was that strange bush, where, sacred
>   fire,
> Religion, did not consume, but'inspire
> Such piety. . . .[40]

Similarly the golden but unfulfilled promises of Raleigh's
Guiana suggest that Fate deals with the English,

> As with the Jewes guide God did; he did show
> Him the rich land, but bar'd his entry in;[41]

while death, the grave, and the life beyond, become the
delivery from bondage and the trek across the wilderness:

> . . . so when our persecutor, our flesh, shall die,
> and the slumber of death shall overtake us in our
> Egypt, His angels . . . shall call and invite us
> from this Egypt to that Canaan. Between which
> (as the Israelites did) we must pass a desert; a
> disunion and divorce of our body and soul, and a
> solitude of the grave.[42]

Of the New Testament, on the other hand, Donne
makes even more sparing use. The stories from the lives of

Christ and the Apostles are, in fact, conspicuous by their absence from his imagery; of the others few merit individual attention. Almost unique in its clear use of a New Testament story is that in which the Countess of Huntingdon's character is illustrated from the tale of the Three Wise Men; her virtue, says Donne, is a light which guides men,

> As such a starre, the Magi led to view
> The manger-cradled infant, God below.[43]

VIII

MYTH AND CLASSICAL STORY

It is hardly necessary to enlarge upon the importance of classical mythology as a source of imaginative embellishment in Elizabethan-Jacobean writing.* The legends of the Gods and human heroes of the ancient world were extraordinarily popular as the subject of verse or prose and for the purpose of illustration and adornment. It was perhaps this very popularity, with its inevitable tendency to stereotype and render stale even the most fanciful of fables and the most inspiring of symbols, that affected Donne. In any case, our evidence seems to indicate that he was definitely reluctant in his verse and absolutely opposed in his prose to making use of those myriad characters and legends without which, some Elizabethan writers seem to have felt, no literary work could be complete.† We look in vain in Donne for images from the tales and deeds of figures almost ubiquitous in the literature of his time; from the celebrated legends, for example, of Jove and Europa or Danae, Venus and Adonis, Orpheus and Eurydice, Daphne and Apollo, Diana and Endymion, Philomela, Procne and Tereus, Tarquin and Lucrece, Perseus and Medusa, and, although he mentions them, Hero and Leander, and Pyramus and Thisbe; from Aeneas, Jason and the Golden Fleece, Helen and Paris, Troilus and Cressida,

---

* See, for example, Douglas Bush, *Mythology and the Renaissance Tradition in English Poetry,* University of Minnesota Press, 1932.

† Miss Beatrice Johnson has attempted to make a case for Donne's interest in such classical matters. The examples she adduces in her paper, "Classical Allusions in the Poetry of Donne" (*PMLA,* XLIII, Dec. 1928, 1098-1109), seem to me for the most part casual and therefore unconvincing.

Hector and Achilles; from the exploits of Hercules; from
the Naiads, dryads, oreads and maenads, the fauns, satyrs,
graces, centaurs and Harpies of classic mythology.

The fact that Donne was undoubtedly well-acquainted
with this entire body of fable makes his meagre use of it all
the more significant. In only a few passages do the images
reveal more than the merest passing interest. One of
these, part of the unrelievedly vituperative attack on
"Julia" in Elegie XIII, summons up Chimera, the sulphur-
ous caverns of Taenarus,* the underworld that is Orcus,
and the Chaos of Greek cosmogony. This Julia is, Donne
declares, a "she Chymera, that hath eyes of fire"; her
breath is like

> the juice of Tenarus
> That blasts the springs;

her mind is

> that Orcus, which includes
> Legions of mischiefs, countless multitudes
> Of formlesse curses, projects unmade up,
> Abuses yet unfashion'd, thoughts corrupt,

and these,

> like those Atoms swarming in the Sunne,
> Throng in her bosome for creation.[1]

The same sense of the word Chaos seems to be present in
Donne's plaintive address to Cupid in Elegie XII:

> tak'st thou pride to break us on the wheel,
> And view old Chaos in the Pains we feel? [2]

and when, in another scurrilous attack on a woman, he
compares the head of another man's mistress to

---

* See *Grierson,* II, 82.

> the first Chaos, or flat seeming face
> Of Cynthia.[3]

The moon-goddess, here rather unceremoniously yoked to
Chaos, serves in a more conventional capacity when Donne
in Elegie XII compares the darkening effect of his beloved's departure to the fading of Cynthia and Venus.[4]

Donne frequently personifies love, but only here and
there does he do so in terms of the classical conception,
as modified by Ovid—that is, of the little winged Cupid
with the dangerous bow and arrows. This is obviously
the source of the metaphor, for instance, when he asserts
that making constancy a virtue has done immedicable
harm to Love and bereft him of

> those awfull wings with which he flies;
> His sinewy bow, and those immortall darts
> Wherewith he'is wont to bruise resisting hearts.[5]

Equally conventional is his use of the traditional symbol
of oblivion, Lethe. Thus he reproaches a friend who, living
in the provinces, tends to forget him, with—

> Your Trent is Lethe; that past, us you forget; [6]

and describes those who have forgotten Elizabeth Drury
as men drowned in a Lethe which makes them forget all
good.[7] Midas, too, appears in his most familiar guise:

> . . . Midas joyes our Spanish journeys give,
> We touch all gold, but find no food to live; [8]

but Hercules, all the specific legends concerning him
ignored, is simply the generalized symbol of power:
". . . wee have a Hercules against these Gyants, these
Monsters; that is, the Phisician. . . ." [9]

Somewhat less familiar are the mythical figments to
which he likens his mistress in Elegie VIII—

> Like Proserpines white beauty-keeping chest,
> Or Joves best fortunes urne, is her faire brest; [10]

and the adornments of women in Elegie XIX—

> Gems which you women use
> Are like Atlanta's balls, cast in mens views,
> That when a fools eye lighteth on a Gem,
> His earthly soul may covet theirs, not them. [11]

If the great legend of the wily Odysseus and his travels is not entirely forgotten, neither is it remembered in a way suggesting a really stimulated imagination. Circe is introduced once when Donne, listening to the inane gossiping courtier in Satyre IIII, exclaims:

> I more amas'd then Circes prisoners, when
> They felt themselves turne beasts . . . [12]

and the Sirens appear several times, including that once in the well-known and forthright

> I sing not, Siren like, to tempt; for I
> Am harsh; [13]

and again, when he describes what he hears at the lips of his mistress—

> there Syrens songs, and there
> Wise Delphick Oracles do fill the ear. [14]

The reputation of Mercury as patron-saint of thieves, the episode of the wooden horse of the Greeks and the lies Sinon told the Trojans can be detected in the epigram which Donne flings at the newsletter, *Mercurius Gallo-Belgicus:*

> . . . Change thy name: thou art like
> Mercury in stealing, but lyest like a Greeke. [15]

But these virtually exhaust the more significant of the figures drawn from Greco-Roman mythology; however, he also uses, although vaguely or fragmentarily, the storminess of the Furies, the thread-spinning of the Fates, the beauty of nymphs, the poetic inspiration of the Helicon, flaming Phaeton and the horses of the Sun, the substitution of Christian temples for those of Jove and Diana, and Darkness (Erebus) pursuing Light (Aether). The several interesting images from pagan sacrificial ceremonies, touched upon in the chapter on images from religion, may also be recalled here.

We may complete the picture of Donne's use of myths by noting the virtual absence of images from fairy lore— that mythology of the Middle Ages already widespread in the literature of Donne's time. He does refer in one place to masquers who have come too late and

<blockquote>
will stay,
Like fairies, till the Cock crow them away; [16]
</blockquote>

and in another to children who

<blockquote>
like Faiery Sprights
Oft skipt into our chamber, those sweet nights; [17]
</blockquote>

but in their casualness these, I think, serve only to set off more plainly Donne's indifference to a tendency that dominated the poetry and prose of his age.

* *

Donne's imaginative interest in Greek and Roman history or the stories popularly connected with characters from that history appears to be no greater than his interest in classic mythology. Hardly more than a handful of the tales, true and fictive, concerning the emperors, heroes, and lovers of classical tradition find a place in his imagery.

Standing uncertainly between myth and history are the Sybils and their mysterious prophetic books. The obscurity of these serves Donne in the raillery he directs at the *Crudities* of that Elizabethan fantastic, Thomas Coryat:

> As Sibyls was, your booke is mysticall; [18]

and their reputation is put to use when he describes to his love how great her future fame will be: I'll tell you, he says,

> How thine may out-endure
> Sybills glory, and obscure
> Her who from Pindar could allure,
> And her, through whose helpe Lucan is not
> lame,
> And her, whose booke (they say) Homer did finde,
> and name— [19]

using thus the fame not only of the Sybils' books but also of several women sometimes associated with three famous poets of antiquity.* That wonder of the ancient world, the Colossus of Rhodes, is called up in Elegie IV by the "grim eight-foot-high iron-bound serving-man" of his beloved's father,

> He that to barre the first gate, doth as wide
> As the great Rhodian Colossus stride; [20]

and elsewhere, somewhat whimsically, by a mandrake.[21] To illustrate the attractiveness and charm possible in age, Donne—by way of tribute to the autumnal beauty of Magdalen Herbert—recalls the tale of a Lydian plane-tree so wonderful in size and age that Xerxes actually bedecked it with gold; [22] and in the epithalamion for Lord Somerset and his bride he expresses the hope that the couple's love may shine,

---

* According to Professor Grierson (*op. cit.*, II, 27) these are probably Corinna who defeated Pindar at Thebes, Lucan's wife Polla Argentaria who is said to have aided him with the *Pharsalia,* and either of two women reputed to have provided the source of Homer's account of the Trojan War—Helena, daughter of Musaeus, or Phantasia of Memphis.

> as in Tullias tombe, one lampe burnt cleare,
> Unchang'd for fifteene hundred yeare.[23]

Somewhat less in the province of doubtful legend are those images which utilize the vanity of Caligula and Messalina, the despotism of Nero, and the tendency of the Romans to naturalize certain provinces only that they might wreak vengeance on them by making them bear the burden of the commonwealth. Probably the most effective of these is that in which, illustrating the evanescence of worldly glory, Donne calls up several moving examples of ancient vanity:

> The very places of the Obelisks and Pyramids are forgotten, and the purpose why they were erected. Books themselves are subject to the mercy of the magistrate . . . Caligula would abolish Homer, Virgil, and all the lawyers' works, and eternise himself and his time in medals: the Senate after his death, melted all them: of their brass his wife Messalina made the statue of her beloved player; and where is that?[24]

I give the entire passage because among other things it is a remarkable anticipation both in content and tone of several parts of Sir Thomas Browne's famous "Hydriotaphia or Urn-Burial". Finally, it may be pointed out by way of conclusion that except for the use in this passage of the monuments of the Egyptians, and a few other figures from the destructive nature of the Goths and Vandals, Donne's imagery reveals virtually no debt to or interest in the events of ancient history.

IX

THE ARTS

The student of imagery taken from the arts by an
Elizabethan writer must keep in mind the fact that there
was throughout Elizabeth's time a certain disparity in the
progress of the various arts. Drama and poetry flourished
as they never had before, the advance of music, although
considerable, was somewhat less spectacular, while painting and sculpture showed only moderate life. In the visual
arts, in fact, England lagged far behind Italy and the
Netherlands, and appreciation of them—in the modern
sense of the word—seems to have undergone no extraordinary development in Elizabeth's time. Naturally Donne's
taste was conditioned by these facts; if they do not explain his interests they at least supply the perspective in
which they must be viewed.

Turning first to his images from music we find that
there are about thirty of them but that they are drawn not
so much from the simple and sensuous aspects of the art as
from technicalities — technicalities having, in some instances, more to do with the physics of sound and the
construction of instruments than with music itself. In
fact, in the few figures that are not concerned with such
technical matters, the only ideas drawn on more than once
are those of harmony and its embodiment in the tuned
instrument. Such a revelatory simile as occurred when he
wrote to Sir Henry Goodere, "Let falshood like a discord
anger you," [1] is unusual; much more typical are such
broad images as that in which he describes the world as
an organ and Elizabeth Drury as one of those spirits which

keep it in tune,[2] or Sir Philip Sidney and his sister, trans-
lating the Psalms, as an organ whereof God himself is the
harmony.[3] Somewhat more particularized is that in which,
seeking to illustrate how God does not destroy just and
unjust indiscriminately, he writes:

> God is a God of harmony, and consent, and in a
> musical instrument, if some strings be out of tune,
> we do not presently break all the strings, but re-
> duce and tune those, which are out of tune;[4]

or that which describes a responsive soul as one who "what-
soever string be struck in her, base or treble, her high or
low estate, is ever tuned to God";[5] and finally, that in the
"Hymne to God my God" which envisions his going to
heaven as an approach

> to that Holy roome,
> Where, with thy Quire of Saints for evermore,
> I shall be made thy Musique; As I come
> I tune the Instrument here at the dore,
> And what I must doe then, thinke here before.[6]

We begin our transition to images from more technical
phases of the art with a figure wherein he declares of an
obsequious fop:

> . . . as fidlers stop lowest, at highest sound,
> So to the most brave, stoops hee nigh'st the
> ground.[7]

Those who substitute reading for thinking evoke a comparison between two long-forgotten forms of music: "To
know how to live by the booke," Donne declares in a letter,
"is a pedantery, and to do it is a bondage. For both hearers
and players are more delighted with voluntary than with
sett musike."[8] The prototype of modern counterpoint, descant, is utilized when he promises a friend he will write

him regularly "though it be but a descant upon this plain song, that I am

> Your affectionate servant
> J. Donne [9]

Such indicators of the length or nature of notes as semibreve and crotchet are used to describe the sermons of Puritan preachers in Problem II or the breath of a sick man in Elegie I; and "division," which Elizabethans understood as a rapid melodic passage wherein each of a succession of long notes was divided into short ones,* appears when he says of the irregular breathing of a dying man,

> Thinke thy selfe labouring now with broken
>   breath,
> And thinke those broken and soft Notes to bee
> Division, and thy happyest Harmonie. [10]

There is, moreover, a small group of images which, in its preoccupation with curious physical phenomena, hardly touches on music at all. The struggles of this world, allegedly dead since Elizabeth Drury's passing, are compared to

> a Lute, which in moist weather, rings
> Her knell alone, by cracking of her strings, [11]

and tackling, snapping in a storm, recalls treble strings "too-high-stretched." [12] Although only distantly related to music proper, two effective figures are that in which he describes mind as those thoughts, affections, and passions which "neither soul nor body hath alone, but have been begotten by their communication, as Musique results out of our breath and a Cornet"; [13] and that in which he assures a friend that his letters convey only intermittent indication of how often he thinks of her,

---

*C. T. Onions, "A Select Glossary of Musical Terms," in *Shakespeare's England,* Oxford University Press, 1917, II, 37.

> As sometimes by the changing of the winde, you
> begin to hear a Trumpet, which sounded long before
> you heard it. . . .[14]

* *

Although Sir Richard Baker records among other
things that young Donne was a "great frequenter of
Playes," * and although Donne himself on one occasion
refers familiarly to the city's theatres—as having been
emptied by the plague,—[15] the only direct comment he
makes in those early years on playwrights and actors themselves is a contemptuous one; in Satyre II he describes a
playwright as one who

> (like a wretch, which at Barre judg'd as dead,
> Yet prompts him which stands next, and cannot
> reade,
> And saves his life) gives ideot actors meanes
> (Starving himselfe) to live by his labor'd
> sceanes;
> As in some Organ, Puppits dance above
> And bellows pant below, which them do move.[16]

It is a little difficult to reconcile this with the remarks of
Baker and Cornwallis unless we interpret this passage as
referring only to hack playwrights and inferior actors.
However, whatever Donne's attitude may have been in
those youthful years, there is little doubt that he came
later to hold plays and playgoing in little regard. Besides
the fact of his position as clergyman, the progressive de-
moralization of the Jacobean stage may have had something to do with this; at any rate, we find him declaring,
after he had taken orders: ". . . because I am drowsy, I
will be kept awake wtih the obscenities and scurrilities of
a comedy, or the drums and ejulations of a tragedy. . . ."[17]

---

* *Chronicle of the Kings of England* (1653), London, 1674, p. 447.

In view of such comments, conflicting as they may be, we are hardly surprised to find that, all in all, Donne's images from the theatre are not impressive and that they appear for the most part in his early writings. Most of those that do turn up in his later work are mere references; one, somewhat longer, suggests that we might well desire to go to heaven to see the saints and martyrs, just as we go to comedies and masks only to see the great there.[18] Most interesting of the figures in his earlier writings are two drawn from the story of Tamburlaine, and therefore probably from Marlowe's famous play. In one he compared the way ships languish in a calm with "Bajazet, encag'd, the shepheards scoffe"; and in the other he wrote:

> I confesse that this is my sicknes worst fitt and as fearefully ominous as Tamerlins last dayes black ensignes whose threatnings none scaped.[19]

Such topical allusions, it may be added, are unusual in Donne's images.

Several other figures from plays are worth noting here; in one he says to Sir Henry Wotton that

> . . . Courts are Theaters, where some men play Princes, some slaves, all to one end, and of one clay;[20]

in another he characterizes men of France as

> the rightest company
> Of Players, which upon the worlds stage be;[21]

and in a third describes the condition of the decks of a becalmed ship as completely disordered,

> Like courts removing, or like ended playes—[22]

a passage which, as Professor Grierson suggests,* seems to

---

* *Op. cit.*, II, 136.

lend support to the idea that Elizabethan stages used more properties than is generally believed. When the Essex expedition was forced back to Plymouth after its first attempt to set out on the Islands Voyage, he wrote:

> The first act of that play which I sayd I would go over the water to see is done and yet the people hisse. How it will end I know not. . . .[23]

and a few lines further on he added, concerning the attitude of the poverty-stricken populace of Plymouth: "Never was exreame beggery so extreamely brave except when a company of mummers had lost theire box."[24] We may mention, finally, several metaphors from the role of the zany, the simpleton mimic of old comedies, and particularly that figure wherein Donne describes the admirers of Lady Huntingdon as so much her zanies that

> no fountaine good there is, doth grow
> In you, but our dimme actions faintly shew.[25]

* *

Although, as I have warned, images from painting and sculpture are scarce, the few that do appear show touches of genuine appreciation and some interest in the fine points of the art. One unusual analogy reveals Donne's reaction to one of the most famous painters of miniatures of his time. Writing to Christopher Brooke he declares that his own lines, when dignified by his friend's judgment, will assume added significance, as

> a hand, or eye
> By Hilliard drawne, is worth an history,
> By a worse painter made;[26]

and in "The Expostulation" he touches upon the artist's joy in work when he compares his desire to renew the times when he first saw love in his beloved's eyes with

Painters that do take
Delight, not in made worke, but whiles they
make.[27]

The sculptor foreseeing the lineaments in the unhewn
stone under his hand is called to mind by the way Christ
foresaw the great possibilities in the fishermen, Simon and
Peter;[28] and the slowness of the painter who follows every
contour before he reproduces a man serves as contrast to
the speed with which the Holy Ghost teaches those whom
he takes in hand.[29]

There is, in addition, at least one peculiar—but typically Donnean—phase to these figures from painting; it
has to do with the way certain portraits appear to stare
back at a spectator regardless of where he stands. This is
just the sort of odd phenomenon to catch Donne's fancy;
he uses it to illustrate how God's image in our souls turns
toward God, how various are the examples offered by
David's life, and finally, how Memory, turned toward God,
finds him always turned toward Memory's possessor.[30]

The question of images from writing and literature
might be approached in several ways. In one sense it might
be said to embrace all figures that have their source in
books, including, for example, a great number of those
already dealt with in other chapters of this study. I preferred, instead, to isolate under this heading only those
figures which seemed to me to issue directly from a sense
of books as books and writing as writing. The result was
more than a score of images coming from such miscellaneous sources as chronicle records, the sizes of books, tex-
tual notes, and the construction of sentences. Most of them
were entirely casual and the whole group was so heterogeneous that any attempt at generalizations or deductions
would have been hazardous. I was able to find only one
figure in which books and writing played an important

role; in Meditation 17 Donne declared:

> All mankinde is of one Author, and is one volume; when one Man dies, one Chapter is not torne out of the booke, but translated into a better language; and every Chapter must be so translated; God emploies several translators; some peeces are translated by age, some by sicknesse, some by warre, some by justice; but Gods hand is in every translation; and his hand shall binde up all our scattered leaves againe, for that Librarie where every booke shall lie open to one another. . . .[31]

THE EVIDENCE
PART II

X

DOMESTIC LIFE

The writer who could produce any considerable body
of writing without imagery from the circumstances of his
domestic life and his immediate environment would be
rare if not unique. Obviously we must expect such imagery, while realizing at the same time that its significance is limited—particularly if it is made up mainly of
commonplace metaphors or images whose figurative quality
can hardly be felt. To convince us that his interest in the
circumstances of his daily life was not entirely conventional or casual a writer's images from this source would
have to be at once recurrent, studied, peculiar to him, and
characterized by a certain amount of imaginative excitement. Donne's work yields a very large number of images
from this source but few of them are distinguished by these
qualities. Here and there, to be sure, he succeeds in
piercing the film of familiarity and revealing in some memorable figure what he has seen behind it, but these, as we
shall see, are the exceptions.

Donne's images from the domestic scene may be considered most conveniently in four groups: houses, the
household itself, clothes, and food. From the first he draws
figures utilizing the various types of buildings, their basic
structure and component parts. In these, for example, we
get glimpses of this world as an inn to the body,[1] the body
as an inn to the soul,[2] the body after death as a completely
deserted house doomed to putrefaction,[3] the brain as the
soul's bedchamber,[4] this world compared with the next as
a country house compared with a palace[5] or as a bed-

chamber compared with a gallery,[6] bodies buried in earth
but with souls in heaven as great buildings with deep
foundations but high turrets,[7] and, finally, this world as
a house, each kingdom a gallery in that house, and church
and state two walls in each gallery.[8] The structure or parts
of buildings appear in such figures as that in which the
beauty that hides bodily decay is described as marble on a
structure made of brick,[9] eyes as lattice,[10] and, in several
places, man's body as a house (or temple) wherein the
bones are timber, beams or rafters,[11] the flesh is loam
walls, the eyes windows, the feet the foundation, the hair
a thatched roof,[12] and the muscles, sinews and veins are
tiles.[13] Only once does he draw an analogy from the actual
mechanics of construction: devotions, he says in this instance, bear us upright even though they have some lean-
ing towards natural affections, as an arch is the strongest
support although it have declinations.[14]

From the household, its familiar activities and furnishings Donne takes many score images but most of these are
commonplace or conventional. However, a sifting of this
large body of metaphor soon reveals several distinct and
curious concentrations of interest. By far the most prominent of these is his imagery from light and fire as provided
by candle, torch, lamp, furnace, and fireplace.* The use of
these as symbolic of that which lives vitally but briefly
produces several vivid, if not entirely original figures;
ringing many changes on this central theme, Donne presents images of the soul as a torch which gives more light
and is warmer than any outside,[15] of God's giving life as
the kindling of light in a lantern,[16] of the flesh as a glass
lantern containing the flame of the heart,[17] of life itself as

---

* An imaginative interest very closely allied to this, that in the light
and shadow created by the sun, is dealt with in "The Heavens," Chapter
XVIII.

a short taper,[18] and of a woman who died young as a

> Lampe of Balsamum, desir'd
> Rather t'adorne, then last. . . .[19]

A striking reversal of this parallel occurs in two images
in which life is seen as a darkness followed by a death that
comes like light: of the dead Elizabeth Drury he wrote:

> Heaven is as neare, and present to her face,
> As colours are, and objects, in a roome
> Where darknesse was before, when Tapers come;[20]

and to his own soul he said:

> Thinke then, my soule, that death is but a Groome,
> Which brings a Taper to the outward roome,
> Whence thou spiest first a little glimmering light,
> And after brings it nearer to thy sight.[21]

Lovers, too, we learn elsewhere, are tapers—which at their
"own cost die." [22] When he says, however, that he himself
as a lover is, in his mistress' hands, a torch ready to be
lit or put out,[23] he verges on the trite—and plunges over
that verge when, in strained tribute to the Earl of Somerset's bride, he writes:

> First her eyes kindle other Ladies eyes,
>   Then from their beames their jewels lusters
>   rise,
> And from their jewels torches do take fire,
>   And all is warmth, and light, and good desire.[24]

In their use of light and fire several images recall vividly
the importance of fire-making in the Elizabethan household routine. In one, speaking of the waste in voracious
but indiscriminate reading, he writes:

> I do therfore more willingly . . . keep awake that
> smale coale which God hath pleased to kindle in mee

> than farr off to gather a faggott of greene sticks
> which consume without flame or heat in a black
> smoother. . . .[25]

in another, the danger of a relapse while he is recovering
from a sickness suggests that man's body is not like the
city, where "when the Bell hath rung, to cover your fire,
and rake up the embers, you may lie downe and sleepe
without feare," [26] and in a third he declares that the whole
world is, in its sins, "a pile of fagots, upon which wee are
laid," and for which ignorance acts as bellows.[27]

Among household objects, as elsewhere, Donne's interest in the clarity of the mechanically precise can easily be
observed. If he peers below the surface of the familiar or
the commonplace it is in quest of unexplored exactnesses,
of realms wherein the subtlest distinctions are perfectly
caught and fixed in the objectivity of some mechanical or
technical relationship. In this case he finds it behind the
familiar face of clock or watch; in fact, before he is
through he has utilized in his imagery every conceivable
phase of clockwork. Will God pretend to make a watch,
Donne asks,

> and leave out the springe? to make so many various
> wheels in the faculties of the soule, and in the or-
> gans of the body, and leave out Grace, that should
> move them? or wil God make a springe and not
> wind it up? Infuse his first grace, and not second
> it with more . . .? [28]

If man is a clock and God the great clockmaker, obviously,
then, death is but a temporary dismemberment; and so he
asks in his elegy for Mistress Drury—

> . . . must wee say she's dead? may't not be said
> That as a sundred clocke is peecemeale laid,
> Not to be lost, but by the makers hand
> Repollish'd, without error then to stand.[29]

Apparently there is no concept so abstract or spiritual that clockwork cannot clarify it. Prayer, he says in one of his sermons, is preceded by meditation and followed by rumination, as "a clock gives a warning before it strikes, and then there remains a sound, and a tinkling of the bell after it hath stricken"; [30] and ritual, he avers in another, moves not God but conserves that order which does move him, as in a watch the string (a clock part now obsolete) moves nothing yet conserves the regularity of the motion of all. [31] But these are hardly more than marginal notes compared to the imagery from clocks and watches that he introduces into his "Obsequies to the Lord Harrington." Here he sees ordinary men as pocket watches which need constant guidance from the great steeple clocks of the world, from men, that is, like Lord Harrington. The former, he says, are small "pocket-clocks"

> whose every wheele
> Doth each mismotion and distemper feele,
> Whose hand gets shaking palsies, and whose string
> (His sinews) slackens, and whose Soule, the spring
> Expires, or languishes, whose pulse, the flye,
> Either beates not, or beates unevenly,
> Whose voice, the Bell, doth rattle, or grow dumbe,
> Or idle, 'as men, which to their last houres come,
> If these clockes be not wound, or be wound still,
> Or be not set, or set at every will;
> So, youth is easiest to destruction,
> If then wee follow all, or follow none.

The great clocks have the real responsibility; they which

> in steeples chime,
> Plac'd to informe whole towns, to'imploy their
> time,

>An error doth more harme, being generall,
>When, small clocks faults, only'on the wearer fall;

but Harrington is the ideal even among the great clocks; therefore, concludes Donne, apostrophizing his subject,

>Why wouldst not thou then, which hadst such
>   a soule,
>A clock so true, as might the Sunne controule,
>And daily hadst from him, who gave it thee,
>Instructions, such as it could never be
>Disordered, stay here, as a generall
>And great Sun-dyall, to have set us All? [32]

There are similar though much less interesting concentrations of imagery on a few other household objects. From mirrors and their optical effects come such a finely shaded figure as

>. . . every creature shows God, as a glass, but glimmeringly and transitorily, by the frailty both of the receiver, and beholder,[33]

the subtle sequence of images describing a calm—

>Smooth as thy mistresse glasse, or what shines
>   there,
>The sea is now,[34]

and the observation, in his verse tribute to Lady Carey and Mrs. Riche, that he must repeat his praise for each of them,

>as in short Galleries
>The Master at the end large glasses ties,
>So to present the roome twice to our eyes.[35]

Sponges are, of course, perfect symbols of the absorptive and as such they occur repeatedly in Donne; occasionally, however, he explores them in his own peculiar manner: "Every man is but a sponge . . . filled with tears," he declares in one place: "and whether you lay your right hand or your left upon a full sponge, it will weep"; [36] and in another he points out that if a rich man is disgraced, endangered, or preferred, it costs him money, just as an overfilled sponge, if pressed, lifted, or moved, gives water—and even dampens the place when it stands still.[37] A bed, on the other hand, appears in most cases as an emblem of death. Openly recognizing the image as image he said to his congregation:

> Thy bed is a figure of thy grave; such as thy grave receives thee at thy death, it shall deliver thee up to judgment at last; such as thy bed receives thee at night, it shall deliver thee in the morning; [38]

and in the burial sermon for Sir William Cokayne he described the grave as a "green-bed, whose covering is but a yard and a half of turf, and a rug of grass. . . ." [39] But probably the most common and prosaic of the actions that he makes use of is that of opening a pack; he applies it, in all its simple realism, to strip the last mystery from the notion of physical death. "Thinke thee," he says,

> laid on thy death-bed, loose and slacke;
> And thinke that, but unbinding of a packe,
> To take one precious thing, thy soul from thence.[40]

In its homeliness this brings to mind a realm of household activities and a species of imagery which Donne failed to explore. One full-fledged example of the type does appear, and it serves to clarify the lack; in it he describes a poor lawyer acquiring lands, painfully, piece by piece,

> as a thrifty wench scrapes kitching-stuffe,
> And barrelling the droppings, and the snuffe,

> Of wasting candles, which in thirty yeare
> (Relique-like kept) perchance buyes wedding
> geare.[41]

There are not many figures of this truly homely kind in
Donne; but it may be pointed out that in most of the
major poets of his time such imagery probably never
occurs at all.

* *

On turning to Donne's images from clothing and food
it is at once evident that while his interest in the latter
is not very considerable at least a few aspects of the
former really stir his fancy. It is probable that his interest in the fashion, quality, and condition of clothes
reflects something of the life he led as the free-living
youth-about-town and, later, as pensioner among courtly
patrons. He writes knowingly when he says:

> sooner may a gulling weather Spie
> By drawing forth heavens Scheme tell certainly
> What fashioned hats, or ruffes, or suits next yeare
> Our subtile-witted antique youths will weare

than an empty-headed London dandy know where or with
whom he is going next. And earlier in this same piece he
describes a whore as one

> who hath beene
> Worne by as many severall men in sinne,
> As are black feathers, or musk-colour hose.[42]

The Elizabethans were notorious for their adventurous
spirit in clothing-fashions as well as in other things: thus
one of Donne's perverse reasons for the desirability of ugly
Flavia is that no one else will covet her, for she is unique
in appearance, while "things in fashion every man will
weare." [43] Style is again the source when he says in Satyre
II that good works are still good,

> but out of fashion now,
> Like old rich wardrops,[44]

while in "The Anagram" he puts the accent on quality,
declaring that unattractive women make good wives, just
as

> For one nights revels, silke and gold we chuse,
> But, in long journeyes, cloth, and leather use.[45]

Consciousness of the condition of clothes is also evident
in "Good Friday, 1613. Riding Westward" when he refers
to the flesh which Christ had worn as "apparell, rag'd and
torne"; [46] when, in a letter, he describes life at court as a
"garment made of remnants, a life raveld out into ends"; [47]
and finally in "The First Anniversary" when, documenting
his theory of the degeneration of the modern world, he
says that even earth's colors have decayed, that

> summes robe growes
> Duskie, and like an oft dyed garment showes.[48]

Besides these we note images which issue from such other
articles of apparel as doublet, cloak, jerkin, scarf, ribbons,
beads, ring, bracelet, spangles, and, we might add, um-
brella, purse, and spectacles. Several interesting figures
come from the making of clothing; two of these are, in
fact, excellent examples of the creative magic by which
he transforms seemingly commonplace materials into vivid,
peculiarly accurate and altogether unique imagery. Describing the ecstatic communion which possessed him and
his beloved as they gazed at each other, he says:

> Our eye-beames twisted, and did thred
> Our eyes, upon one double string; [49]

and seeking in "The Second Anniversary" to make clear
the almost mystic instantaneousness of Elizabeth Drury's
transportation to heaven, he says:

> . . . speed undistinguish'd leads
> Her through those Spheares, as through the
> beads, a string,
> Whose quick succession makes it still one thing.[50]

In both instances a theme transcendently spiritual is illuminated by a practical, even prosaic detail of domestic life, but the point of parallel is so unusual and yet so apt that the total effect of the image is electrical.

Donne's images from food are, as I have said, much less varied than those from clothes, and reveal no particular interests. In fact, only a few of them may be said actually to involve the sense of taste itself. Among these few are that in which he says: "An office is but an antepast, it gets them an appetite to another office; and a title of honor, but an ante-past, a new stomach to a new title"; [51] and that in Paradoxe I where he declares that women would rather enjoy all the virtues distributed among several men than "confused" in one, on the grounds that the latter is as tasteless as divers meats minced together in one dish.[52] At the end of a very thoughtful, almost sombre letter to Sir Henry Goodere, he writes:

> These, Sir, are the sallads and onions of Micham, sent to you with as wholesome affection as your other friends send Melons and Quelque-choses from Court and London; [53]

and in another place the way the English improve on the sins they import from other nations reminds him of how a "weaker grape growing upon the Rhine, contracts a stronger nature in the Canaries." [54] Candied garden stalks, or "angelica," a delicacy once familiar, now rare, are utilized in

> So controverted lands
> Scape, like Angelica, the strivers hands; [55]

and the growing popularity of the apricot—once rare, now familiar—serves him when he asserts:

> . . . Jesuits are like Apricocks, heretofore here and there one succour'd in a great man's house, and cost deare, now you may have them for nothing in every cottage.[56]

In the remaining figures of this group Donne draws on the obvious symbolism in the leavening and kneading of dough, the mellowing and fermenting of liquors, the chafing and pressing of grapes, in bread, meat, lard, wine, spirits, syrup, the shelling of nuts, in curded milk, jelly, spices, and mustard seed, and in such processes as chewing, swallowing, regurgitating, and digesting. But remembering the considerable body of poetry and prose from which they are taken, these images from food and taste reveal if anything the relative unimportance of this sense as a source of Donne's imagery; there is obviously no element here of the discerning palate of a Shakespeare, the lush sensuousness of a Keats.

All these throw light on the nature of Donne's interests; except for one facet, however, they are less significant concerning the way his imagination operates in making use of them in his writing. That one aspect refers to the small but striking group of images from clocks, mirrors, and needle-threading; these figures make clear that although the sources of an image may be prosaic and familiar, its application, if sufficiently imaginative and unusual, can completely transfigure its effect. In their utilization of the least obvious aspects of the familiar such figures reveal a tendency clearly allied to that which turned him toward unfamiliar or recondite sources. By means of both types he avoided the really commonplace, striking out figures which he could be quite sure had not been used before. In both, moreover, the reader experiences almost equally the exhilaration involved in following that sudden and exciting movement of intellect and imagination which occurs as a writer perceives and develops a significant relationship between two ideas where no such relation was ever perceived before.

XI

SPORTS AND GAMES

Concerning the sports and pastimes that interested most Elizabethan and Jacobean writers we know all too little. Among all the data that we may secure from autobiographical passages or the biographical notes left by their contemporaries these activities usually receive the least attention. Therefore it is in such a direction that imagery offers us, I feel, really luminous clues. It may not be able to fill in the entire picture but it can certainly furnish us with a goodly number of significant details.

In Donne we find, all in all, no considerable imaginative interest in outdoor life or indoor sports. That he was acquainted with most of these and appreciated the fine points of a few is clear; but there is little indication that he was an ardent follower of such activities in general or a thorough student of any particular one. If there are any which may be said to have attracted his fancy particularly, they are the allied pastimes of falconry and fowling. In one of the most arrogantly libertine passages in his songs he explains how he has gained complete control over love:

> Thus I reclaim'd my buzard love, to flye
> At what, and when, and how, and where I chuse;
> Now negligent of sport I lye,
> And now as other Fawkners use,
> I spring a mistresse, sweare, write, sigh and
> weepe:
> And the game kill'd, or lost, goe talke, and sleepe.[1]

Here the image from bird-training is called to mind by

the poet's mastership over love; in another it is suggested by God's mastership over death; to the latter Donne says:

> though thou beest, O mighty bird of prey,
> So much reclaim'd by God, that thou must lay
> All that thou kill'st at his feet, yet doth hee
> Reserve but few, and leaves the most to thee.[2]

In a third, the way man may be held to vanity, even if only by a silken thread, suggests the eagle which "though she enjoy her wing and beak, is wholly prisoner if she be held by but one talon." [3] Even the lay reader can follow these; on the other hand, almost wholly a part of the mysteries of hawk-training is the figurative aspect of the assertion that "both want and abundance equally advance a rectified man from the world, as cotton and stones are both good casting for an hawke." [4] The same holds true for the practice of seeling—that is, sewing up a bird's eyes while training it—which he utilizes in several figures: those who soar intellectually until heaven humbles them, he explains in a sermon, are seeled birds that fly upwards till their strength is spent.[5] The idea of catching birds by net and snare, which appears in several of his metaphors, may owe as much to Biblical imagery as to the sport itself, but the use of lime for the same purpose probably harks back to actual fowling practice. Casting bird-lime serves to describe, on the one hand, women who expose their bodies and paint themselves,[6] and, at the other extreme, prayers directed toward attaining God's mercies.[7] Once, apparently mocking the speech of a typical court gallant, he wrote:

> He call'd her beauty limetwigs, her haire net;
> She feares here drugs ill laid, her haire loose set,[8]

yet he himself used both "limetwigs" and "nets" in several metaphors.[9]

From the other two most popular Elizabethan pastimes, hunting and angling, there are less than a dozen images. One in which he declares that statesmen "hunt their fortunes, and are often at default: Favorites course her and are ever in view," [10] is interesting in the precise distinction it makes between hunting and coursing (the pursuit of the hare by greyhounds, by sight, as distinct from hunting) ; and another, describing the utter hopelessness of becalmed sailors—

> for here as well as I
> A desperate may live, and a coward die.
> Stagge, dogge, and all which from, or towards
> flies,
> Is paid with life, or pray, or doing dyes,— [11]

offers among other things an extreme example of Donne's use of ellipsis. The remaining figures from hunting are commonplace, and those from fishing are entirely negligible. In the light of the lack of interest that this would seem to indicate it is an ironic fact that Donne's most reverent and sympathetic biographer should be Izaak Walton, by far the most famous celebrater of the joys of angling.

From the many sports popular throughout Donne's lifetime we find only a scattering of images. Whether he was ever attracted to these can hardly be decided with certainty but that they no longer stirred interest in him by the time he came to do the bulk of his writing seems evident. We note several analogies from archery, fencing, wrestling—

> men big enough to throw
> Charing Crosse for a barre,— [12]

from bowling—

> Women . . . by the mastery of some over-ruling
> churlish husbands, are forced to his Byas, yet have

they a motion of their own, which their husbands never know of. . . .[13]

and from horsemanship, foot-racing, football, and "baloune".* Tennis appears in two interesting figures, one referring to the Earl of Arundel as "that tennis ball whome fortune after tossing and banding brikwald into the hazard"; [14] and the other describing a friend's affection as having been secured indirectly, through other friends, "by way of reflection or Briccole . . . to use the Metaphor of a Game." [15] Of competitive indoor games there is virtually nothing. Any expectation that Donne's penchant for subtleties and mental gymnastics might lead—especially in his later years—to such a game as chess, is disappointed; he used it once, coldly and distantly, referring to courtiers as sorry creatures

> Whose deepest projects, and egregious gests
> Are but dull Moralls of a game at Chests.[16]

Although he alludes to span-counter and blow-point in Satyre IIII, the only boys' games that occur in his images are bubble-blowing and stool-ball. The former makes several appearances the most vivid of which is that in the comparison between the dangerous thinking of those who meditate too much on evil and

> those toyes
> Of glassie bubbles, which the gamesome boyes
> Stretch to so nice a thinnes through a quill
> That they themselves breake. . . . [17]

---

* Identified by *Grierson* (II, 124) as a game played with a large windball struck with arm or foot.

XII

SEA TRAVEL AND EXPLORATION

With the Thames the most popular of local thoroughfares and with sailors scattered throughout the city, the average Londoner of Elizabeth's day could hardly help knowing something of ships and sea travel. Moreover, when he went abroad he did so under circumstances which brought him into such contact with sailing life as no liner-passenger of today can ever come. The significance of this becomes clear when we learn that Donne not only went abroad but travelled so extensively that several of his friends actually thought of him as a traveller.* We know, for example, of a tour of the Continent (ca. 1595–1596) which took him to Italy and Spain (and was intended, says Walton, to carry him even to the Holy Land), of a trip to Paris with Sir Robert Drury in 1611–1612, and of his attending Lord Doncaster's embassy through Europe to Germany in 1619–1620. These were essentially by land; much more important, from the point of view of naval experience, were his volunteer enlistments with the two famous expeditions of the Earl of Essex. The first reached Cadiz and sacked it, but the second, the Islands Voyage, which aimed to intercept the rich Spanish plate-ships, met such a storm that it was ignominiously driven back to Plymouth, and finally reached the Azores only after many difficulties. Of the miseries of that sorry retreat before the storm we get a vivid picture in the mordant, rugged, and metaphor-packed lines of "The Storme" and "The Calme,"

---

* See John Sparrow's "The Date of Donne's travels," pp. 123–151 in *A Garland for John Donne,* ed. Theodore Spencer, Harvard, 1931.

the two best-known of Donne's verse letters, and in a prose letter written from Plymouth in the interval between attempts to set sail. Even elsewhere in his writing we find passages like

> dar'st thou lay
> Thee in ships woodden Sepulchers, a prey
> To leaders rage, to stormes, to shot, to dearth? [1]

and—just after he has referred to "Spanish journeys"—

> To mew me in a Ship, is to inthrall
> Mee in a prison, that weare like to fall;

and

> Long voyages are long consumptions,
> And ships are carts for executions. [2]

Such in brief was Donne's experience with ships. It is enough to prepare us for one of the main currents of his imagery from this source—the tendency to recall the more unpleasant aspects of sea travel and to consider all such travel as symbolizing progress through any medium beset with countless and inexorable perils. For almost every difficulty of life Donne found vivid counterpart in the experience of the seafarer. "Every thing refreshes, and I wither," he wrote to Sir Henry Goodere in a moment of despondency,

> . . . and being to passe more and more stormes, I finde that I have not only cast out all my ballast which nature and time gives, Reason and discretion . . . but I have over fraught my self with Vice, and so am riddingly subject to two contrary wrackes, Sinking and Oversetting. . . . [3]

When his mother suffered tribulation he applied the figure to her life, describing it as a sea under a continual tempest, wherein the way had been "strait, stormie, obscure". [4]

Several times he envisoned all life as such a journey; in the last prayer of his *Devotions* he wrote:

> Though the rockes, and the sands, the heights, and the shallowes, the prosperitie, and the adversitie of this world do diversly threaten mee, though mine owne leakes endanger mee, yet, O God, let me never put my selfe aboard with Hymeneus, nor make shipwracke of faith, and a good conscience; [5]

and, summing up homiletic-wise in a verse letter to Sir Henry Wotton, he said:

> Life is a voyage, and in our lifes wayes
> Countries, Courts, Towns are Rockes, or
> > Remoraes;
> They breake or stop all ships. . . . [6]

If life is a voyage, it follows that death is the disaster that stops it short; in a passage which resembles a Hamlet soliloquy in the tortuous indecision of its musings, Donne wrote:

> I would not that death should take me asleep. I would not have him meerly seise me, and onely declare me to be dead, but win me, and overcome me. When I must shipwrack, I would do it in a Sea, where mine impotencie might have some excuse; not in a sullen weedy lake, where I could not have so much as exercise for my swimming. Therefore I would fain do something; but that I cannot tell what, is no wonder. For to chuse, is to do: but to be no part of any body, is to be nothing. [7]

Such a figure as this seems to me a good example of those images which are least of all merely embellishment, which are, in fact, so integral a part of meaning that they may well be considered the inevitable statement of it.

Images from the most wretched aspects of ship-life—
from tempest, fire, shipwreck and scourge—leap to
Donne's mind again and again. In one place a man who,
beaten by life and in danger of betraying his soul, puts
off his body, is a tempest-tossed ship which throws off most
of its wares to save its passengers;[8] and, in another, one
who relies on a woman is a mariner who anchors under a
rock and runs the danger of being beaten against it.[9] Occasionally the figure suggests the seamanlike procedure in
such dangers. The church, he says in a sermon, may, if
necessary, give up her means of ease and propagation but
never her basic articles, as in tempests men cut down gal-
leries, tear up cabins and hew down the mast itself, but
never touch the keel;[10] and once, speaking of the disputes
concerning the authorship of Genesis, he observed:

> Therefore, as in violent tempests, when a ship dares
> bear no main sail, and to lie still at hull, obeying
> the uncertain wind and tide, puts them much out of
> their way . . . it is best to put forth such a small
> rag of sail as may keep the bark upright and make
> her continue near one place, though she proceed
> not; so in this question. . . .[11]

The various kinds of sea-sickness left vivid memories
and these suggest the comparison between men who de-
scend to embracing an idolatrous worship and seasick
sailors who would rather be trodden upon than rise up;[12]
and between those who do not carry their share of man's
burdens and sailors who steal away in a calenture or
scurvy.[13] All the miscellaneous misfortunes of the sea seem
to have made their impress on his imagination: a firebrand
that burns most desperately when cast into a state accus-
tomed to peace calls to mind the fire which razes the ship
at sea sooner than a thatched house;[14] admirers are said

to stand in the same relation to a patron as fleets to the sun—they "perish too farre off, and burne too nigh"; [15] storm-tattered sails recall the cruelest punishment at sea, for from such

> sailes, ragges drop downe so,
> As from one hang'd in chaines, a yeare agoe; [16]

and, finally, the difficulties arising from the way he has settled all his love on a particular woman can be described only in terms of bad loading—

> Whilst thus to ballast love, I thought,
> And so more steddily to have gone,
> With wares which would sinke admiration,
> I saw, I had loves pinnace overfraught. [17]

At least once, however, Donne used a sea disaster as if it were nothing if not a thing of beauty. On the Azores voyage he may conceivably have come upon the peak of Teneriffe breaking from the sea and towering into a moon-lit sky.* Once seen, it was a vision not to be forgotten. "Doth not a Tenarif," he was to ask in after years,

> Rise so high like a Rocke, that one might thinke
> The floating Moone would shipwracke there,
>   and sinke? [18]

This use of the idea of shipwreck is, I think, a superb instance of what the poet's imagination can do with the harshest of realities.

There are, to be sure, images in this group without any dolorous overtones; such, for example, is that in which he says that the world continues to move after Elizabeth Drury's death only

---

* See *Grierson*, II, 191, concerning the possibility that Donne did not come near enough to descry the peak on either of his two expeditions.

> as a ship which hath strooke saile, doth runne
> By force of that force which before, it wonne; [19]

or that a man's way of life indicates with what intentions he comes to sacrament—just as the "spread and swoln" sails and the ship's direction reveal to the sailor the invisible wind.[20]

But the interesting thing about this group is that the only sizable cluster of related images in it, besides those with distressful implications, are the figures drawn from the use of the compass and various technical phases of navigation. Our acquaintance with Donne's experience among ships may have prepared us in some measure for the images out of unhappy memory; it does not prepare us for the considerable interest he shows in the compass. Our conclusion—if I may anticipate the actual evidence—must be that this imaginative interest (already observed in several other chapters) in precision instruments and things technical or merchanical simply transcends any unpleasant context that these may have had in actuality. They so suit the natural bent of his fancy that nothing else seems to matter. Thus one of the few images that lights up and lends imaginative life to the uninspired pages of the *Essays in Divinity* is that which discovers and explores the parallels between faith and a navigator's compass. Those who seek God through "reason and natural strength," he declares, are

> like mariners which voyaged before the invention of the compass, which were but coasters, and unwillingly left the sight of the land;

but now faith has come, and,

> as by the use of the compass, men . . . have found out a new world richer than the old; so doth faith

> . . . direct and inform in that great search of the discovery of God's essence. . . .

His figure is already complete, but his imagination has dwelt too long on the notion of the compass to abandon it thus easily; so he adds:

> . . . though the faithfullest heart is not ever directly, and constantly upon God, but that it sometimes descends also to reason; yet it is not thereby so departed from Him, tho not fully to Him: as the compass is ever Northward, though it decline, and have often variations towards East and West.[21]

The technicalities of navigating by the pole-star furnish several figures which verge on the recondite. We are guided spiritually, he says in one of them, by that which is nearest to God, His Church, just as

> by the selfe-fix'd Pole wee never doe
> Direct our course, but the next starre thereto,
> Which showes where the'other is, and which we say
> (Because it strayes not farre) doth never stray;[22]

and in the other, speaking of man's inevitable weaknesses, he declares:

> A compass is a necessary thing in a ship, and the help of that compass brings the ship home safe, and yet that compass hath some variations, it doth not look directly north; neither is that star which we call the north-pole, or by which we know the north-pole, the very pole itself; but we call it so, and so we make our uses of it . . . because it is the nearest star to that pole. He that comes as near uprightness, as infirmities admit, is an upright man, though he have some obliquities.[23]

Again we note in passing the looseness and diffuseness of the prose image as compared with the one in poetry.

In his almost inexhaustible eulogizing of Elizabeth Drury there are few sources which Donne did not succeed in using; navigation is not of these few for in "The First Anniversary" he describes the dead girl as

> She whom wise nature had invented then
> When she observ'd that every sort of men
> Did in their voyage in this worlds Sea stray,
> And needed a new compasse for their way.[24]

And finally—utilizing an observation of the compass as apt as it is unusual—there is that image in which he tells men that though they may suffer aberrations in bending their will to God, in Him alone can they hope for rest— just as the compass needle, though it may shake and shake, comes at last to rest looking toward the pole.[25]

We come now to two figures, issuing from the professional practice of the navigator, which take rank among the most uncompromisingly technical in Donne. In one he asserts that we can best judge the greatness of love when we remain in its presence but that absence alone can indicate how long it will last, just as

> To take a latitude
> Sun, or starres, are fitliest view'd
> At their brightest, but to conclude
> Of longitudes, what other way have wee,
> But to marke when, and where dark eclipses
> bee?[26]

and in the other, lamenting the shortness of Lord Harrington's life on earth, he says:

> Thou knowst, that though the tropique circules have
> (Yea and those small ones which the Poles
> engrave,)

All the same roundnesse, evennesse, and all
The endlesnesse of the equinoctiall;
Yet, when we come to measure distances,
How here, how there, the Sunne affected is,
When he doth faintly worke, and when prevaile,
Onely great circles, than can be our scale.[27]

In the first of these he refers to the ascertaining of a latitude by "measuring the distance from the zenith of a star whose altitude, i. e. distance from the equator, is known," and longitude by the difference between the time of the occurrence of an eclipse at the first meridian and at the ship's position; * and in the second he alludes, in "tropique circles," to those which run parallel to the equator and are smaller near the poles, and, in "great circles," to those which run from pole to pole.† It should be noted that these almost dismayingly complicated and precise scientific figures are applied—particularly in the first case—to the most common and elementary of human relationships and feelings.

EXPLORATION

Exploration by land and water had been going on for hundreds of years but the Elizabethan-Jacobean era saw its really great florescence. The sagas of those who ventured with Renaissance curiosity and boldness across uncharted seas into the unknown beyond were enough to stir any man's imagination, and few writings of the time are without some reference to the exploits they record. Not only was the whole story of these epics of travel made available in the great compilations of Eden, Hakluyt, and

---

* See *Grierson*, II, 29.
† *Ibid.*, II, 208.

Purchas, but Donne, in addition, came into contact with the very movement itself, for on both Essex expeditions Raleigh—already connected with the Guiana ventures—played a prominent part. Thereafter, comments on Raleigh or Guiana are recurrent in Donne's writings—from the epigram, "Cales [Cadiz] and Guyana," addressed to Raleigh and Essex when they were debating where next the fleet should sail, to the sharing of Sir Walter's visionary hopes which Donne reveals in a verse letter to Rowland Woodward.*

Furthermore, another connection with this movement may be seen in the fact that in 1609 Donne sought to be Secretary at Virginia, that in later years he was called to preach a missionary sermon on the Virginia Indians to the Honourable Company of the Virginia Plantation, and that he may even have been, according to Gosse, one of the shareholders in this enterprise.† Finally, an interesting direct reference to exploration occurs in *Ignatius His Conclave* when Donne introduces Columbus as claiming—along with such other memorable disturbers of the established order of things as Copernicus, Paracelsus and Machiavelli—a place next to Lucifer, and describes him as one who "having found all waies in the earth, and sea open to him, did not feare any difficulty in Hell." [28] Although Ignatius, in accordance with his role, goes on to ridicule Columbus, Donne's respect for the Genoese explorer is clear, and we are hardly surprised to find that the images stimulated by the discovery of America and the possibility of a shorter passage to the East are the most prominent in this group.

The first of these is called up in the Elegie "Going to

---

* *Grierson*, I, 210, ll. 18-28.

† *Op. cit.*, I, 209 and II, 162.

Bed" by the joys of a lover's explorations. "Licence may roaving hands," he cries,

> and let them go,
> Before, behind, between, above, below.
> O my America! my new-found-land.[29]

He has much the same idea in mind when he says to his beloved

> Let sea-discoverers to new worlds have gone,
> Let Maps to other, worlds on worlds have showne,
> Let use possesse one world, each hath one, and
> is one;[30]

and when he compares the way faith, superseding reason, had enabled men to attain God's essence with the way the compass had enabled navigator's to find "a new world richer than the old." [31] Once, recalling tales of Spanish cruelty in the New World, he says that those at Court who are armed only with virtues are like Indians facing Spaniards [32]—a comparison issuing as much from hatred of the Spanish as from sympathy with the savages. Elsewhere Donne even recognizes the spiritual kinship between the Raleighs who were pushing into the wastes of the New World and the Galileos who were venturing into those of solar space; in a verse letter to Lady Bedford he uses them as parallel symbols of man's almost godlike power to augment his universe:

> We'have added to the world Virginia, 'and sent
> Two new starres lately to the firmament;
> Why grudge wee us (not heaven) the dignity
> T'increase with ours, those faire soules
> company.[33]

The routes, both actual and conjectured, to the East served Donne in several ways. Thus the blindness of the people of earlier ages to new ways of reaching God must have been suddenly rendered clear and vivid to his hearers when he asked them:

> Who ever amongst our fathers, thought of any other way to the Moluccas, or to China, than by the promontory of Good Hope? Yet another way opened itself to Magellan; a strait, it is true; but yet a way thither; and who knows yet, whether there may not be a north-east, and a north-west way thither, besides? [34]

Writing in his loftiest vein to Lady Huntingdon he asserts that passion may lead a man to a woman but something is necessary if her love is really to be won and held,

> As all discoverers whose first assay
> Findes but the place, after, the nearest way; [35]

and, in another place, speaking—with notable liberality of attitude—of the equal efficacy of different religions, he says: "Men go to China, both by the Straights, and by the Cape." [36]

Again and again among these images we find the "East" and "India" serving as symbolic of all that is precious and desirable. Such, for example, is virtue, and such too—as we might expect—are patronesses like Lady Bedford and Elizabeth Drury. In Elegie XVIII, "Loves Progress," it becomes the goal of the love-maker's explorations; here, in one of the longest and most circumstantial of the figures in his poetry (it continues for more than thirty lines) Donne describes the lover as setting out, ship-like, from his beloved's head and proceeding downward. He crosses her brow which, when smooth, becalms him, but, when wrinkled, shipwrecks him, and comes to the nose, a first meridian running—somewhat confusingly—between two suns, the eyes, with hemispheres, the cheeks, on both sides. The meridian directs the voyager to those "ambrosial" islands, the lips, from between which come Siren songs and Delphic oracles. The mouth is a creek in which dwells that cleaving remora, the tongue; below is the promontory of the chin and then the "streight Hellespont between the Sestos and Abydos of her breasts." A boundless sea dotted with island moles succeeds, and then a forest, place of shipwrecks. Although the desired India is then not far, few reach it.[37]

Fantastic as this analogy may seem it is not without parallel in the poetry of the age: Shakespeare in *The Comedy of Errors* (Act III, Scene ii) makes Dromio describe the kitchen maid in much the same terms, and Phineas Fletcher not only saw the human body as an island but his bizarre book-length elaboration of topographical details, *The Purple Island,* makes Donne's figure seem simple and succinct by comparison.

Scattered through Donne's imagery are other items connected directly or indirectly with the records of exploration: the storminess of the Bermudas, the Mediterranean as transition between two worlds, the energy of the Russian merchants (who came to London after the Willoughby and Chancellor expeditions to "Muscovy"), and that epitome of all that is opposite—the Antipodes.

* *

In considering Donne's images from navigation we saw how he was led—almost without consciousness, I venture to say—toward the technical niceties of the compass; so in these images from exploration we find another curious direction, another semi-technical field mined for the peculiarly accurate, mechanically precise parallels to experience that it can provide. In the "Hymne to God my God" the physicians who study his body are seen as mapmakers poring over their work. My physicians are grown cosmographers, he says,

> and I their Mapp, who lie
> Flat on this bed, that by them may be showne
> That this is my South-west discoverie
> *Per fretum febris,* by these streights to die,
>
> I joy, that in these straits, I see my West;
> For, though theire currants yeeld returne to
> none,
> What shall my West hurt me? As West and
> East
> In all flatt Maps (and I am one) are one,
> So death doth touch the Resurrection.[38]

Here, once again, the Straights of Magellan play their part, but it is to the last idea, the odd fact that on a globe the farthest west and the farthest east from any point merge and become identical, that he returns fascinatedly, again and again. "Take a flat map, a globe *in plano,*" he says in one of the sermons,

> and here is East, and there is West, as far asunder as two points can be put: but reduce this flat map to roundness, which is the true form, and then East and West touch one another, and are all one: so consider man's life aright, to be a circle, *Dust thou art, and to dust thou must return.* . . .[39]

The image is presented here in the deliberate, almost dilatory manner characteristic of Donne's images in prose; in his poetry its counterpart is a succinct, single-line aside, as when he says of the falling of the Annunciation and the Passion on the same day:

> this day hath showne,
> Th'Abridgement of Christ's story, which makes
> one
> (As in plaine Maps, the furthest West is East)
> Of the'Angels *Ave,* 'and *Consummatum est.*[40]

Elsewhere, the way in which the east becomes west when a map is fitted to a ball serves to illustrate how a troubled soul can become peaceful by being made to conform to the gospel; [41] and even heaven is a map with two hemispheres wherein America is the glory reserved for later discovery.[42]

If we go beyond the images specifically connected with exploration and examine those drawn from foreign lands in general, we find them sparse and surprisingly colorless. Outside those frequent allusions to the richness of the East which we have already considered, and which are for the most part related to exploration, few call for detailed attention. We note in passing minor figures referring to the heat of Etna, the noise made by scolding Sclavonians, the changeable nature of Frenchmen, the dark complexion of Moors, the roar of Sicilian vault fires, the queerness of China's manufactures, and the rareness of "faire houses" in Holland owing to its distance from woods and quarries. Except that they appear to echo rumor as much as fact and suggest an attraction to the more peculiar aspects of things exotic, these yield little that is significant.

XIII

COMMERCE AND COINAGE

It is axiomatic, I suppose, that commerce, trade, and coinage are unpoetic. Their code is practical, their goal material; it is traditional, therefore, to place them in opposition to the things which allow freedom to the fancy and give life to the more tender emotions. Yet Donne's images from this source are fairly numerous and sometimes surprisingly vigorous. The use of a source presumably prosaic and even crass may be considered another facet of Donne's rejection of the Petrarchian and Spenserian conventions. The significant fact here is not that Donne shows any more than average knowledge of commercial matters—it is simply that he uses such materials to throw light on things conventionally supposed sacred to the spirit.

There is, one might even say, a kind of perversity in the metaphor he chooses when he writes to a friend, ". . . I was sure, you took not up your Religion upon trust, but payed ready money for it, and at a high Rate," [1] or when, writing on a theme no less holy than the thoughts of Christ that came to him when the Annunciation and the Passion fell on the same day:

> This treasure then, in grosse, my Soule uplay,
> And in my life retaile it every day, [2]

or when, addressing God himself, he said:

> Father, part of his double interest
> Unto thy kingdome, thy Sonne gives to mee,
> His joynture in the knottie Trinitie
> Hee keepes, and gives to me his deaths conquest. [3]

Less daring, perhaps, but almost as challenging is his approach to love in the same terms: "Did you draw bonds to forfet?" he asks a fickle mistress in "The Expostulation," "signe to breake?" [4] To another he declares that his treasure (of letters and oaths), calculated to purchase her, has been spent,

> Yet no more can be due to mee,
> Then at the bargaine made was ment;

that now, moreover, there will be rivals who

> . . . have their stocks intire, and can in teares,
> In sighs, in oathes, and letters outbid mee; [5]

and in his epithalamion for Princess Elizabeth and Count Palatine he describes passion as a coin in which lovers are rich—

> They quickly pay their debt, and then
> Take no acquittances, but pay again. [6]

Tenantry and rent furnish such figures as that in which he speaks of his fevers as a rent which he pays regularly—and earlier with each year; [7] and life as a short lease followed by one which lasts a thousand years. [8] "Wee are but farmers of our selves," he writes to his friend Woodward,

> yet may,
> If we can stocke our selves, and thrive, uplay
> Much, much deare treasure for the great rent
> day; [9]

and in Meditation 8 he says of man:

> . . . of the happinesses of this world hee is but Tenant, but of misery the Free-holder; of happines he is but the farmer, but the usufructuary, but of misery, the Lord, the proprietary. [10]

His most considerable interest, however, appears to be in trade by sea and from foreign lands—an interest linked, of course, with that in travel and exploration. Again we may note in at least half a dozen figures the use of "western treasure and eastern spicery" or the gold of the West and the perfumes of the East as symbolic of all that is most desirable. Thus, for example, the man bent on fortunes in this world and therefore not interested in resurrection is compared to one who has plenty and cares not about perfumes in the East or gold in the West Indies.[11] Advising a friend to save up his country pleasures and bring them to the city, he says:

> as plenteously
> As Russian Marchants, thy selfes whole vessel
>   load,
> And then at Winter retaile it here abroad;[12]

and probing another concerning the effects that taking religious orders may have had on him, he asks:

> as a Ship after much paine and care,
> For Iron and Cloth brings home rich Indian ware,
> Hast thou thus traffiqu'd, but with farre more
>   gaine
> Of noble goods, and with lesse time and paine?[13]

Privateers assailing merchantmen richly laden with a dyestuff like cochineal is the background of the analogy when, satirising the creatures of the Court, he says:

> The Ladies come; As Pirats, which doe know
> That there came weak ships fraught with
>   Cutchannel,
> The men board them;[14]

and finally, reaching a peak in his juxtaposition of the holy and the worldly, is his comparison of Christ paying with his life to redeem mankind from Satan with

> a robb'd man, which by search doth finde
> His stolne stuffe sold, must lose or buy'it
> againe.[15]

Turning from commerce to other kinds of vocations and occupations—and to the human types involved in them—we find an extremely varied group of images presenting a miscellany of allusions to the work of smith, carpenter, enameller, surveyor, carver, lapidary, clockmaker, wire-drawer, engraver, potter, glassblower, jeweller, steel-glass maker, commissary, steward, statuary, broker, secretary, and notary, and to such mechanicals as watchman, porter, servant, waggoner, and knifegrinder. There is no concentration of interest on any one of these, but in several images there may be seen, if but faintly, evidence of that tendency toward the technical and the subtly esoteric of which we have already taken note. Thus he declares in his *Essays in Divinity* that those who dispute and cavil over Scripture are like such lapidaries as can "spy the flaw, but not mend it with setting"; [16] and the way Christ foresaw the potentialities in the fishermen Simon and Peter, suggests the ability of these same lapidaries to foresee the possibilities in a rough stone.[17] A jeweller fashioning a jewel into a flower or an emerald symbol is the delicate figure which illuminates how the Holy Ghost moves a man in certain directions; [18] and the subtle, mysterious way Christ uncovers Christ in man is uniquely figured in carvers who

> do not faces make,
> But that away, which hid them there, do take.[19]

THE SYMBOLISM IN COINS

We find in many Elizabethan writings a curious interest in coins and coinage; in Donne that interest assumed the proportions of a mild obsession. There is hardly a phase of this subject—whether the mining of the metal, the storing of ingots, the actual minting, the royal stamp, the uses and values, the wear, the debasing, clipping, or counterfeiting—that Donne's several score images do not explore in some detail. And there are very few matters of the spirit, whether holy or profane, which he does not succeed in illuminating by means of it.

Among the most frequent of these images are those using the idea of the official stamp or impression which gave coins their currency. At parting from his beloved he says:

> Let me powre forth
> My teares before thy face, whil'st I stay here,
> For thy face coines them, and thy stampe they
> beare,
> And by this Mintage they are something worth; [20]

eleswhere he speaks of his mistress as she

> Whose faire impression in my faithfull heart,
> Makes mee her Medall, and makes her love mee,
> As Kings do coynes, to which their stamps
> impart
> The value; [21]

and in "The Second Anniversary" he says of Elizabeth Drury:

> Shee coy'nd, in this, that her impressions gave
> To all our actions all the worth thy have.[22]

In another passage—in a discussion of a kind unusual in his sermons—Donne declares that in all metrical compositions of the type exemplified by the Book of Psalms

> the force of the whole piece, is for the most part left to the shutting up; the whole frame of the poem is the bearing out of a piece of gold, but the

last clause is as the impression of the stamp, and
that is it that makes it current; [23]

and in the *Essays in Divinity* he describes devotion in
similar terms, saying:

> . . . we fetch part of our wealth, which is our
> faith, expressly from his treasury, and for our good
> works, we bring the metal to His mint . . . and
> the impression of His grace, makes them current
> and somewhat worth. . . . [24]

Again, seeking analogy for the change effected in Tilman
by his taking of orders, Donne finds it in that which new
kings do to old coins: You are, he says to his friend,

> as before,
> Onely the stampe is changed; but no more,
> And as new crowned Kings alter the face,
> But not the monies substance; so hath grace
> Chang'd onely God old Image by Creation,
> To Christs new stampe, at this thy Coronation. [25]

The relation or contrast between the value of different
coins gives rise to another series of parallels. The heathens,
he observes in "The Second Anniversary," took the attributes of their one true God, turned them into lesser deities,
and

> by changing that whole precious Gold
> To such small Copper coynes, they lost the old,
> And lost their only God. . . . [26]

This figure remained with him, and years later he used it
again, with minor changes, in a sermon. [27] The reverse
mutation, from base metal to gold, would be miraculous—
and therefore serves perfectly when he compares God's
opening the graves and freeing men at resurrection with
the issuing forth as talents of gold that which was once
only copper money. [28]

Clipping, defacement, and debasement, prove again and again to be useful sources of imagery. In one figure the taking away of a book of Scripture is seen as a clipping of God's coin; and in another Christ is a coin stamped with God's image and man a rusty copper with the same image defaced by many sins.[29] Of the amalgam that is happiness Donne writes:

> . . . scarce any happiness that hath not in it so much of the nature of false and base money, as that the Allay is more then the Metall;[30]

and of virtue in certain kinds of men:

> . . . as money is not called base, till the allay exceed the pure; so they are vertuous enough, if they have enough to make their actions currant, which is, if either they get praise, or (in a lower abasing) if they incurre not infamy or penalty.[31]

Counterfeiting serves equally well: In one passage Donne describes spiritual comforts as gold stamped by God and temporal ones approved by God as silver also stamped, but other worldly comforts as man's counterfeit coining of copper;[32] and in another God is declared to be as much offended by an adulterer as by an idolater or a blasphemer, just as the law is broken equally by a man who coins a penny as by one who makes a larger coin.[32]

We can hardly expect to sample all the phases of Donne's imaginative excursions into the world of coin; one more must suffice: During his brief stay among the poverty-ridden people of Plymouth, he wrote:

> I should thinke wee were in utopia: all are so utterly coyneles.[34]

The ideal state, abolishing coins and thereby all the processes from minting to clipping, would also eliminate one of the most prolific of the sources of Donne's imagery.

XIV

KING, STATE, AND WAR

Throughout his life Donne numbered among his friends and patrons many persons of the noblest rank and most eminent official position in the kingdom. He held intimate correspondence with men like Sir Henry Wotton, did service for officials like Elizabeth's Lord Chancellor, Sir Thomas Egerton, and could even claim an acquaintance with James himself; it must, in fact, be clear to any reader of his biography that he had ample opportunity to observe at fairly close range the ways of sovereigns and courts and the workings of the state. However, although in later years he became the famous Dean of a great Cathedral and Chaplain in Ordinary to the King, he was throughout the first half of his career a needy retainer compelled to spend his days in pathetic attempts to find a place for himself. Among the multiplicity of circumstances which may have determined his attitude, those unfortunate years certainly deserve an important place. It is not too much, I think, to suspect that this ignominious relation to the court up to the time of his ordination had not a little to do with the fact that in his imagery from king and matters of state he draws again and again on the more unsavory circumstances connected with both. Whatever be the reason, tyranny, treason, espionage, and oppression, play a conspicuous part in this group of images.

On two occasions, seeking to characterize the insidiousness of the affliction known as "vapours," he turns for analogy to sedition. These vapours, he says, which we consider in ourselves

> pestilent and infectious fumes, are in a State infec-
> tious rumors, detracting and dishonourable Calum-
> nies, Libels. The Heart in that body is the King;
> and the Braine, his Councell; and the whole Magis-
> tracie, that ties all together, is the Sinewes, which
> proceed from thence. . . . What Fugitive, what
> Almes-man of any forraine State, can doe so much
> harme as a Detracter, a Libeller, a scornefull Jester
> at home? [1]

and again, using the fact that these vapours may be more
dangerous than diseases having more obvious symptoms—

> Twentie rebellious drums make not so dangerous a
> noise, as a few whisperers, and secret plotters in
> corners. . . . The disease hath established a King-
> dome, an Empire in mee, and will have certaine
> *Arcana Imperii*, secrets of State. . . . But yet
> against those secret conspiracies in the State, the
> Magistrate hath the rack; and against the insensible
> diseases, Phisicians have their examiners; and those
> these employ now.[2]

In "The Anniversarie" Donne and his beloved are kings,
yet like none that reign on earth, for they can ask,

> Who is so safe as wee? where none can doe
> Treason to us, except one of us two;[3]

in Elegie I, on the other hand, his mistress is another's
wife and if they make love in her home, that is, her husband's realm, they are in danger; if, however,

> as envious men, which would revile
> Their Prince, or coyne his gold, themselves exile
> Into another countrie, 'and doe it there,

> Wee play'in another house, what should we
> feare?
> There we will scorne his houshold policies,
> His seely plots, and pensionary spies.[4]

At least two images go so far as to cast reflection openly
on royal worth. In Satyre II the poor lawyer, degraded by
circumstance, must

> to every suitor lye in every thing,
> Like a Kings favourite, yea like a King; [5]

and in one of the Meditations, having described the heart
as king of the principality of the body, he says that even
brain and liver are its subjects and, though they be

> in eminent Place and Office, must contribute to
> that . . . as all persons to all kinds of Superiours,
> though oftentimes . . . those Superiours, bee not
> of stronger parts, then them selves, that serve and
> obey them that are weaker. . . .[6]

If Donne believed that "divinity doth hedge a king" his
imagination seems to have betrayed him in his images.
Several are even definitely suggestive of the particular
kinds of difficulties and afflictions that beset some of the
monarchs of his time. In *Ignatius His Conclave* (published in 1611) when Lucifer shows himself loath to accept
Ignatius' advice lest Ignatius become too important, Donne
observes that he behaves like

> Princes, who though they envy and grudge, that
> their great Officers should have such immoderate
> means to get wealth; yet they dare not complaine
> of it, lest thereby they should make them odious
> and contemptible to the people . . .[7]

a figure limning exactly the relation that existed between
Elizabeth and such a noble as Lord Essex, Donne's com-

mander of other days. In another, of uncertain date, the poet describes what happens when his mistress' father enters the room where he is hidden and smells his perfume:

> . . . like a tyran King, that in his bed
> Smelt gunpowder, the pale wretch shivered— [8]

as an English soverign might well shiver after Guy Fawkes and the Gunpowder Plot of 1605; and in a third he alludes by way of a clever though perhaps not original pun to the crowns of France—both coins and kings—as so lean and worn-looking that they appear to be possessed by "their naturall Countreys rot." [9] Hardly more attractive are the associations behind such figures as that in which the soul summoned by death is described as a traitor who dares not return home; [10] or sorrow as "tyrant, in the fift and greatest Monarchy"; [11] or the surly fellow who replies only "yea" or "nay" as being

> as mute
> As an old Courtier worne to his last suite. [12]

One other figure in this group calls for attention. The idea which it serves to illuminate—that his love grows greater with each spring and lessens no whit in the wintry season that follows—is a beautiful one. To his contemporaries it would have suggested many images, images drawn no doubt from nature, the seasons, or sources considered equally appropriate for such a theme; to Donne it suggested something very different, for he wrote:

> And though each spring doe adde to love new
>   heate,
> As princes doe in times of action get
> New taxes, and remit them not in peace,
> No winter shall abate the spring encrease, [13]

and challenged the epithets "prosaic" and "remote" for
the sake of a fresh, precise, and uniquely illuminating
parallel.

Of the remaining several score images involving royalty
or the state, the greater number make use of the more
obvious attributes of prince, court, throne, crown, kingdom, and province; a few draw upon such details as the
general pardon at the king's coming, the coronation, foreign conquests, the king giving audience, privileged spies,
the alliance of rulers, the presenting of gifts to the sovereign, the moving of court, and the cantoning of a monarchy into states. Only one gives us anything like an
intimate glimpse of these things; in it a plant is described
as forcing itself up through the earth,

> Just as in our streets, when the people stay
> To see the Prince, and have so fill'd the way
> That weesels scarce could passe, when she
>   comes nere
> They throng and cleave up, and a passage cleare,
>   As if, for that time, their round bodies
>   flatned were;[14]

and again the conventional relation of ideas is reversed
and what is seemingly the most prosaic of activities, the
crush of a street mob, illustrates a wonder of nature, the
upward struggle of a young shoot.

Only one figure makes any real attempt to utilize the
abstract functions of government. In "The Second Anniversary" he describes Elizabeth Drury as a state which
enjoyed

> All royalties which any State employ'd;
> For shee made warres, and triumph'd; reason
>   still
> Did not o'rthrow, but rectifie her will:
> And she made peace, for no peace is like this,

That beauty, and chastity together kisse:
She did high justice, for she crucified
Every first motion of rebellious pride:
And she gave pardons, and was liberall,
For, onely her selfe except, she pardon'd all:
Shee coy'nd, in this, that her impressions gave
To all our actions all the worth they have:
She gave protections; the thought of her brest
Satans rude Officers could ne'r arrest.
As these prerogatives being met in one,
Made her a soveraigne State; religion
Made her a Church; and these two made her all.[15]

I give the passage in its entirety as one of the few extended images in Donne's poetry which strike me as having been elaborated for form's sake alone; it reveals at almost no point the intellectual energy which usually vitalizes even the most hyperbolic of the poet's sentiments.

WAR

To Englishmen of the sixteenth and seventeenth centuries war was an integral and unquestioned part of life. When a Milton had such respect for its uses and importance that he could define education as "that which fits a man to perform justly, skilfully, and magnanimously all the offices, both private and public, of peace and war," and a Bacon could assert unqualifiedly that "for Empire and Greatnesse" nations must, above all, "professe Armes, as their Principall Honour, Study, and Occupation," we should hardly be surprised to find that few of the writers of the time escaped its influence and an intimate knowledge of its practices. Moreover, in Donne's case this influence probably came through every one of the possible sources — including not only the treatises (of which there were a vast number published in the second half of the sixteenth century), the local train-bands, and the soldiers returned from campaigns against the Irish, in aid of the Dutch insurgents in the Netherlands and of the French Protestants in France, but also his own service—essentially naval though it was—at Cadiz in 1596 and at the Azores in 1597. The point is that, in view of all these influences, any less than a great variety of images from this source can hardly be thought to indicate any considerable imaginative interest.

Once again love acts as core for a cluster of images from a single source. There are not many such figures but taken together they make up what Donne himself might have called the imagery of love's warfare. In Elegie XX, which he entitled "Loves Warre," Donne says to his mistress:

> Till I have peace with thee, warr other men,
>
> . . . .
>
> All other Warrs are scrupulous; Only thou
> O fayr free Citty, maist thyselfe allowe
> To any one;

and having considered such "other warrs" as those in Flanders, France, Ireland, and Spain, he renounces them, exclaiming:

> Here let mee warr; in these armes lett mee lye;
> Here lett mee parlee, batter, bleede, and dye.
> Thyne armes imprison me, and myne armes thee,
> Thy hart thy ransome is; take myne for mee.
> Other men war that they their rest may gayne;
> But wee will rest that wee may fight agayne;

and

> There Engins farr off breed a just true feare,
> Neere trusts, pikes, stabs, yea bullets hurt
>   not here,

concluding finally—

> Thousand wee see which travaile not
> To warrs; But stay swords, armes, and shott
> To make at home; And shall not I do then
> More glorious service, staying to make men? [16]

The last part of this figure is, of course, more than anything else a fanciful play on words, type of that imaginative exercise called by Elizabethans "evaporations of wit".

Several images represent Love as warlike or violent.
In "The Broken Heart" he comes like sudden death on the
battlefield:

> By him, as by chain'd shot, whole rankes doe
>   dye; [17]

in "The Extasie" the lovers themselves are "two equall
Armies" between which fate "suspends uncertaine vic-
torie"; [18] and in "Loves Exchange" Love is the ruthless
conqueror and Donne the beleaguered town:

> Small townes which stand stiffe, till great shot
> Enforce them, by warres law condition not.
> Such in loves warfare is my case,
> I may not article for grace,
> Having put Love at last to shew this face.[19]

It is enlightening to contrast with this image one wherein
Donne is again a town, but this time in the hands of the
arch-enemy, Satan, and praying for deliverance by God:

> I, like an usurpt towne, to'another due,
> Labour to'admit you, but Oh, to no end,
> Reason your viceroy in mee, mee should defend,
> But is captiv'd, and proves weake or untrue.[20]

The only other theme which repeatedly calls up images from war is sickness. Since sickness is the occasion of the *Devotions* this association is a recurrent one in its pages. Thus in Meditation 10 he describes vapour sickness as a bomb which blows up a wall, other diseases being merely cannon that pound it; [21] in the next he asserts that the brain and liver will hold out longer than the heart, that they will "endure a Siege," but that an "unnatural heat, a rebellious heat, will blow up the heart, like a Myne, in a minute;" [22] and in others he variously describes sickness as a "rebellion of the body" or a cannon which "batters all, overthrowes all, demolishes all." [23] In the most protracted of these analogies he complains that in sickness

> we are but upon a defensive warre, and that is but a doubtfull state; especially where they who are besieged doe know the best of their defences, and doe not know the worst of their enemies power; when they cannot mend their works within, and the enemie can increase his numbers without. O how many farre more miserable . . . than I, are besieged with this sicknesse, and lacke their Sentinels, their Physitians to watch, and lacke their munition, their cordials to defend, and perish before the enemies weaknesse might invite them to sally. . . . In me the siege is so farre slackned, as that we may come to fight, and so die in the field. . . . [24]

In several places he envisons all life as an armed conflict. To Sir Henry Wotton he writes that in this world's warfare those who are so hated by God's "commissary," Fate, as to be placed in the Court's "squadron" are helpless if their only weapons are virtues; [25] and in the *Essays in Divinity* he describes the world as a battle wherein God is the Lord of Hosts, and where, as in "the imperial armies," there are even three *Signa Militaria*, that is, *Signa Vocalia*, the commander's word, "which office the word of God doth to us"; *Semivocalia*, the sound of trumpets and other instruments, in which office we have traditions and sermons; and *Signa Muta*, colors and ensigns, as to us are the creatures and works of God.[26]

It is, moreover, an interesting fact that of the scant handful of images in *Pseudo-martyr* the four most noteworthy come from war. Having been involved, ever since his employment by Bishop Morton, in the furious assault on the Catholics in general and the Jesuits in particular, Donne had, by the time of the publication of *Pseudo-martyr* in 1610, obviously come to think of the schism as a pitched battle. Two of these images make use of the historically momentous change from long-bow to artillery: in one he compares with this shift in weapons the Jesuits' substitution of such peremptory methods as massacre for the circuitousness of excommunication; and in the other he says that the impetuous rage of the Jesuits has stirred up such defences that they convert fewer and fewer—as artillery and gunpowder * have stimulated such protections against themselves that wars kill fewer than ever before.[27] Elsewhere he draws a parallel between the way the Jesuits use any argument to defend their position and men throwing straw and feathers as well as timber and stone into a breach; and finally, identifying each unit in the analogy, he describes James' attempt to make the Catholics take the Oath of Allegiance as a war in which the clergy and universities which defended him were the "pressed men," the obscure villagers who did the same, the

---

* In Satyre II (ll. 19-20) Donne makes an interesting direct comment on this change in arms:

> Rammes, and slings now are seely battery,
> Pistolets are the best Artillerie.

"voluntaries," those who neglected the oath's defense, guards asleep in the castle, and the attacks of the adversaries, "batteries and underminings." [28]

It should no longer be surprising to us to find that Donne prefers to explore strange byways, to unearth unusual metaphors, or at least to use the commonplace in uncommon ways. In this instance he turns to the movement of bullets and the percussion and flare that accompanies explosion; and uses them with scrupulous exactness. Think that death liberates you from the body, he says to his soul in "The Second Anniversary,"

> that a rustie Peece, discharg'd, is flowne
> In peeces, and the bullet is his owne,
> And freely flies. . . .[29]

and in "The Dissolution," associating virtually the same ideas, he insists that although his beloved has died before him, his soul

> more earnestly releas'd,
> Will outstrip hers; As bullets flowen before
> A latter bullet may o'rtake, the pouder being
> more.[30]

Using the detonation of a cannon more in its relation to physics than as a symbol of war, Donne in one place describes a whale's strokes as making "more circles in the broken sea"

> Then cannons voices, when the aire they teare;

and in another tells Lady Bedford not to care how low her praisers be, for

> ordinance rais'd on Towers, so many mile
> Send not their voice, nor last so long a while
> As fires from th'earths low vaults in Sicil Isle.[31]

Powder itself and its explosive action is drawn upon in several places: In "A Nocturnall upon S. Lucies Day" he observes:

> The Sunne is spent, and now his flasks
> Send forth light squibs, no constant rayes; [32]

and in "The Broken Heart" he cynically remarks that talking of a love that continued for any length of time is like saying that one has seen "a flaske of powder burne a day." [33] Similarly, thinking of the explosion of powderballs, he speaks in "The Litany" of "light squibs of mirth," and in "Newes from the very Countrey" chooses "squib" to describe the fortunes of those at Court who "cannot stay at the highest, nor return to the place which they rose from, but vanish and weare out in the way." [34]

Of the remaining images in this group almost all are casual figures referring in tangential or incidental ways to shot, batteries, armory, ransom, citadel, ambush, swords, poisoned arrows, bucklers, and outworks. Among the few carried further than allusion are that in which the bells rung at the passing of a soul and again the following day at the services for the body suggest to him that man is like a marching army whose "Vaunt may lodge to night where the Reare comes not till to morrow"; and that in which the continuity from earth into heaven of the sense of salvation is seen as a lit train of powder that runs into a city and sets fire to it. [35]

Remembering Shakespeare's images from war one is conscious of the absence from this group of all such figures as draw, for example, on the habits and life of soldiers, on the strategy of armies, and the activities of individual soldiers on the actual field of battle. The sense of men's relation to the things of war is throughout exceedingly faint.

XV

METALS AND SUBSTANCES

Turning to Donne's images from metals and substances, we approach them, I think, with the expectation that they will tell us something concerning the writer's sensory reactions—as Professor Spurgeon learned, by the examination of similar sources, of Shakespeare's interest in the texture of things and Marlowe's attraction to their gleam and glitter. But any such expectation meets with disappointment, for Donne's imagination, we soon find, takes an entirely different direction. Converting what might have been an excursion into sense impressions into the outlines of another image-treatise on the technical, he turns not to the feel or appearance of metals and substances but to theories concerning their properties and nature. It is a tendency that fits perfectly into the pattern we have already discerned.

Although the images on which this chapter is based will ostensibly be dealt with as they fall under the headings of metals (or minerals) and substances, we actually find that the first of these narrows itself down to a study of Donne's figures from gold; for Donne in his imagery seeks out the precious yellow metal like an Elizabethan explorer and expounds its virtues with the zeal of an early economist. We have already observed in the chapters on "Medicine and Alchemy" and on "Commerce and Coinage" the conspicuous part played in Donne's imagery by theories involving this metal—particularly in the section on the alchemical transmutation of base metals and in that on mintage and the relative values of coined metals—but

here again, in this concentration of images on the nature
and properties of gold itself, we get a small, almost esoteric field of human interest yielding a host of analogies;
and since the material thus introduced is often prosaic,
fairly technical, and shot through with fine discrimina-
tions in matters of theory, it contributes its share to the
tendency of Donne's poetry to appeal to the intellect rather
than the senses. Such a passage as the following, wherein
he evolves a comparison between the function of women
and that of gold, illustrates most trenchantly how technical—and incidentally how ingenious—such an image
can be:

> . . . preferr
> One woman first, and then one thing in her.
> I, when I value gold, may think upon
> The ductilness, the application,
> The wholsomness, the ingenuitie,
> From rust, from soil, from fire ever free:
> But if I love it, 'tis because 'tis made
> By our new nature (Use) the soul of trade.[1]

The essential parallel here is between preferring a woman
for one characteristic and gold for one attribute, but the
reason for preferring gold, use, has itself an applicability
to woman that is hardly accidental and that is quite typical in its teetering between ingenuity and mere extravagance. But this image may be said to make some use of a
commercial function of gold; much more reliant on the
metal's natural properties are those images which draw
on gold's basic formation, ductility, fusility, tensile
strength, lustre or—most frequent of all—malleability,
its extraordinary capacity to be beaten to any thinness.
It is this property that really fascinates the poet. At
least twice he speaks directly of it: No fire, he wrote in a
verse letter,

> nor rust can spend or waste
> One dramme of gold, but what was first
> shall last,
> Though it bee forc'd in water, earth, salt, aire,
> Expans'd in infinite, none will impaire;[2]

and in a sermon:

> . . . no metal enlarges itself to such an expansion,
> such an attenuation as gold does, nor spreads so
> much, with so little substance.[3]

Any kind of gradual attenuation or dissipation seems to
have called this figure instantly to mind. God's justice
overwhelming all indiscriminately,[4] oversubtle speculations in divinity,[5] religion frittered away by impertinent
questionings,[6] honor becoming tenuous as it spreads,[7] the
capacity of God's word to cover meanings[8]—all are illustrated by some slight variation of the notion of gold being
beaten to leaf. The most effective of the metaphors Donne
bases on this idea, and one which helps to make "A Valediction: forbidding mourning" one of the best known of
Donne's lyrics, varies this association slightly in that gold
leaf is used to suggest not so much an attenuation as an
expansion that is infinite:

> Our two soules therefore, which are one,
> Though I must goe, endure not yet
> A breach, but an expansion,
> Like gold to ayery thinnesse beate.[9]

It is another noteworthy example of Donne's ability to turn
up uniquely satisfactory analogies in the most unusual
places.

Another recurrent association among these images is
that of gold and virtue. This in itself appears to be a
commonplace association—especially when it is used to

describe the attributes of patronesses,—but in most instances Donne succeeds in modifying and individualizing it. When he associates it with Lady Bedford's goodness, it is that unique metal no dram of which rust or expansion can ever impair; [10] when the virtue is God's, it is described as a Western hemisphere full of the metal; [11] if it is shallow or partial, it is substance merely gilt or "informed"; [12] if it passes into narrow men, it is sound gold ingot drawn into wire.[13] But by far the strangest of the kinds of gold that Donne utilizes is electrum, a metallic compound much discussed by ancient alchemists; they defined it as essentially gold, with a small part silver, and as sometimes endowed with magic powers. In comparing Elizabeth Drury's soul with her body it proved to be of unrivalled suitability for it enabled Donne to say:

> Shee, of whose soule, if we may say, 'twas Gold,
> Her body was th'Electrum, and did hold
> Many degrees of that . . .[14]

In comparison with the exceptional variety and subtle probing of these images from gold those from other metals fade into insignificance. Occasional use is made of the dampness, hidden wealth, or "centrique" position of mines; of lead's inertness, iron and its sheath of sin-like rust, of steel and the loadstone which awakens it, of quicksilver's beadiness and steel's resistance, of silver, and of refining processes—the mould, metal red-hot or molten or cooling, —but only a few of these are other than buried or casual.

Standing somewhat apart from these, although they too issue from the earth, are gems. It seems only natural to expect that these, the rarest and most treasured of substances taken from earth, should produce brilliant and unusual imagery; and the memory of many passages in which poets have registered their reactions to precious stones bolsters the expectation. Explain it how you will, Donne's use of these is virtually negligible. The only gems actually named in his images are diamonds, turquoise, saphires, rubies (or carbuncles), and chrysolite. The majority of these, along with a host of other extremes of panegyric, is evoked by Elizabeth Drury, and none goes further than an allusion. It is almost as if Donne, having discovered the poetic possibilities in things thought prosaic, had lost almost all interest in the conventionally poetic. Of the few figures from gems, the most felicitous, as one might expect, makes use of no ordinary point of view. Seeking a counterpart for the impossibility of deciding in what part of the sacrament grace is, Donne finds it in the futility of the eye's trying to assign the place whence lustre arises from a precious stone.[15] It is but another of those many searching images in which Donne sought with curious persistence to illustrate varieties of the impossible.

Pearls, too, play a minor role here—but almost never in their usual capacity as the ideal of purity and of the unblemished. Of all the attributes of pearls that a writer's imagination might seize upon, Donne chooses the pleasantly quaint notion that they are composed of successive shells of hardened dew [16] and the dangerously quaint one that they have medicinal value.[17] Minor as such a choice may seem, it is another item in support of the idea that Donne's turning to the technical and the inobvious—for in most images these two characteristics seem to coincide —is a consistent tendency.

Our second division in this chapter, "substances," turns out to be essentially residual, containing what remains after substances which have been made into special articles have been included under such specific headings as "clothes" or "coinage." The substances left after such repeated sub-dividing—cork, wax, amber, ice, clay, sand, earth, stone, dust, cinders—are apparently not of the type, at least when considered in their most rudimentary forms, that lends itself to striking or unconventional metaphor. There are, however, two vivid exceptions worth noting. In one of them all our categories from gold to substances are straddled in a series of succinct metaphors; speaking, as it were, from below the gravestone, Donne in his epitaph "On Himselfe" says:

> Parents make us earth, and soules dignifie
> Us to be glasse, here to grow gold we lie; [18]

and in the other he declares, with his usual elegiac exuberance, that the only effect death can have on the body of Lady Marckham is to refine her flesh, alembic-like,

> As men of China, 'after an ages stay,
>   Do take up Porcelane, where they buried
>   Clay.[19]

Even if Donne had known that such a conception of porcelain's origin was more striking than accurate, there is little reason to believe that he would have altered it. The quasi-scientific was as much to his purpose as the scientific; and in any event vividness was a much more important criterion in choosing an image.

XVI

MEN AND CHARACTERISTICS

At the heart of a writer's awareness of the life around him are the images he draws from the types of human beings and from human attributes and functions.* They are an essential aspect of that which lends humanity and the quickening sense of life to his work. Although it is probable that no writer is without a trace of such imagery, we may have, at one extreme, the writer who, whether because unworldly or bookish or absorbed in nature, has only a minimum from such a source, and, at the other, he who is more intensely interested in human beings than anything in book or nature and finds in men and their attributes an inexhaustible source of vivifying analogy.

Donne belongs to neither extreme. In more than one chapter we have seen evidence, fragmentary as it may have been, of his keen observation of men and their ways. We have met in his imagery—to mention only the most conspicuous—astronomer, mathematician, physician, apothecary, alchemist, lawyer, thief, judge, prisoner, clergyman, warrior, sailor, sportsman, actor, artist, king, courtier, and artisans and workmen of every kind. These were dealt with in terms of the particular fields of activity of which they are an integral part; we have now to add to them images first from that colorful and heterogeneous host of men and women who belong to no special group,

---

*This, it should be noted, includes personification, which is simply the distinctive name given to such images when they are applied to inanimate things or abstractions. For a full consideration of the metaphoric function of personification see Stephen Brown's *The World of Imagery,* Chapter VI.

and, second, from human characteristics and functions in general.

There is first such a group of images as comes from the family and the ages of man. A few examples will serve to illustrate the extent — or rather the limitations — of Donne's awareness in this direction: In "The First Anniversary," describing the decay of the modern world, he says:

> the Springs and Sommers which we see,
> Like sonnes of women after fiftie bee; [1]

and when Magdalen Herbert was gracious enough to read his verses, he saw her as

> a mother which delights to heare
> Her early child mis-speake halfe uttered words. [2]

How quickly men tire of love is figured by children at a fair; there

> His highnesse sitting in a golden Chaire,
> Is not lesse cared for after three dayes
> By children, then the thing which lovers so
> Blindly admire, and with such worship wooe; [3]

and in Satyre I the society-aping Londoner who can only gesticulate to passing acquaintances because he is walking to the inside of Donne reminds him of

> schoole-boyes which doe know
> Of some gay sport abroad, yet dare not goe. [4]

If the young get little attention from Donne, the old he forgets almost entirely; once, the world dwelling on memories of Mistress Drury is compared to aged men who

> are glad
> Being tastlesse growne, to joy in joyes they had. [5]

But it is apparent that young and old alike and the various ages of man leave Donne, imaginatively speaking, unmoved. A group that did seem to attract his interest and leave him with vivid impressions were the strumpets, beggars, and nondescript creatures typical of the streets of a great city. And in their frankness and vigor the images from this group contribute largely to that strain of realism which runs through much of Donne's verse and particularly his Satyres. In Satyre I, describing the flightiness of a fop, Donne introduces two such analogies; sooner, he asserts,

> may a cheap whore, who hath beene,
> Worne by as many severall men in sinne,
> As are black feathers, or musk-colour hose,
> Name her childs right true father, 'mongst all
> those,

and sooner

> may a gulling weather Spie
> By drawing forth heavens Scheme tell certainly
> What fashioned hats, or ruffes, or suits next yeare
> Our subtile-witted antique youths will weare;
> Then thou, when thou depart'st from mee,
> canst show
> Whither, why, when, or with whom thou
> wouldst go.[6]

In Satyre III he says to those given over to the pursuit of earthly things that the very world they love is

> In her decrepit wayne, and thou loving this,
> Dost love a withered and worn strumpet . . .[7]

and in Satyre II, administering what is apparently the ultimate in insults, he charges that those who practice law merely for gain are worse than "imbrothel'd strumpets prostitute." [8]

The beggars who cluttered London streets find themselves clearly reflected in the glass of these images: to Thomas Woodward Donne wrote that in anticipation of receiving letters from him he lived both in hope and in fear,

> As in our streets sly beggers narrowly
> Watch motions of the givers hand and eye,
> And evermore conceive some hope thereby;

and, having received such a letter, Donne completes the picture, adding,

> And now thy Almes is given, thy letter'is read,
> The body risen againe . . .
> And thy poore starveling bountifully fed.[9]

In "Newes from the very Countrey" atheists in difficulty are "blind beggers . . . forced to aske though they know not of whom";[10] and in another passage afflictions in general are beggers who "tell others, and send more after them."[11]

A striking concentration of such parallels from human types occurs in Satyre III when he sees the various religious which attract men as so many different kinds of women. Mirreus, he says, loves the rags which an old woman left in Rome; Crantz loves her

> who at Geneva is call'd
> Religion, plaine, simple, sullen, yong
> Contemptuous, yet unhansome;

Graius stays at home and

> Imbraceth her, whom his Godfathers will
> Tender to him, being tender, as Wards still
> Take such wives as their Guardians offer;

careless Phrygius abhors all, as one who, "knowing some women whores, dares marry none"; and Graccus loves all, believing that

> As women do in divers countries goe
> In divers habits, yet are still one kinde,
> So doth, so is Religion.[12]

Curiously, in Holy Sonnet XVIII he again sees religion in terms of women, but this time in personifications of a more conventional order. Which is the true church, he asks,

> . . . She, which on the other shore
> Goes richly painted? or which rob'd and tore
> Laments and mournes in Germany and here?[13]

Of more respectable if lowly callings—but almost as familiar sights on London streets—were grooms and bellmen; from them Donne draws a few extremely vivid figures. One of these is that arresting personification of death—

> Thinke then, my soule, that death is but a Groome,
> Which brings a Taper to the outward roome,
> Whence thou spiest first a little glimmering light,
> And after brings it nearer to thy sight;[14]

another describes Donne himself in his sickness:

> . . . I shall be in this world like a porter in a great house, ever nearest the door, but seldomest abroad: I shall have many things to make me weary, and yet not get leave to be gone;[15]

and a third, picturing as a bellman the preacher who tries to prepare his congregation for the music of the messengers of death, declares:

> . . . remember that as in that good custom in these cities, you hear cheerful street-music in the

winter mornings, but yet there was a sad and dole-
ful bellman, that waked you, and called upon you
two or three hours before that music came.[16]

A few others in the motley throng of these images
catch the eye: the poet starting his studies after his youth
is likened to those "giddy travelers" who

> stray or sleepe all day, and having lost
> Light and strength, darke and tir'd must then
> ride post; [17]

his own "Paradoxes and Problemes" are but "swaggerers:
quiet enough if you resist them"; [18] those who sue to
patrons are "singers at doores for meat"; [19] nobility is the
"huffing braggart"; [20] to lovers the rising sun is a "busie
old fool" and a "sawcy pedantique wretch"; [21] the law is a
fair maid with "foule long nailes"; [22] and the sinner's
heart is a miser's bag of money which will not be opened
till death.[23]

The Human Attribute

There are, in addition to these, a body of images of
which the source is not a particular type or class of human
beings but man himself, his body, functions, and normal
characteristics. Among the most vivid of these are several
personifications wherein, although no specific type of per-
son is drawn upon, things inanimate or of the spirit are
imbued with all the vitality of living, breathing beings.
The idea of death, for example, gives rise to three of the
most evocative and suggestive of these personifications.
"Death is in an olde mans dore," Donne says in Meditation 7, "he appeares, and tels him so, and death is at a
yong mans backe, and saies nothing. . . ." [24] "My noble

sister," he writes to Mrs. Cokayne, "I am afraid that Death will play with me so long, as he will forget to kill me . . ." [25] and in a letter to Sir Henry Goodere he begins: "I would not that death should take me asleep. I would not have him meerly seise me, and onely declare me to be dead, but win me, and overcome me." [16] In another (quoted in full as epigraph to this text), as impressive in its own way as these, and rising in a flight as soaring and swift as any in his writing, Donne sees man's thoughts as the vastest of the creatures which this world knows—creatures that are "borne Gyants; that reach from East to West, from Earth to Heaven, that doe not onely bestride all the Sea, and Land, but span the Sunn and Firmament at once. . . ." [27]

There are, of course, a considerable number of personifications of a kind that could probably be found in most Elizabethan and Jacobean writers. Typical examples of these—that is, of the more elaborate and conventional sort—occur in Elegie VI; in one passage he speaks of a stream which

> Doth with doubtfull melodious murmuring,
> Or in a speechlesse slumber, calmely ride
> Her wedded channels bosome, and then chide
> And bend her browes, and swell if any bough
> Do but stoop downe, or kisse her upmost brow— [28]

and continues in this artificial vein through more than a dozen lines; and in the other, lending human attributes to both a whirlpool and a candle, he writes:

> So, carelesse flowers strow'd on the waters face,
> The curled whirlepooles suck, smack, and embrace,
> Yet drowne them; so, the tapers beamie eye
> Amorously twinkling, beckens the giddie flie,
> Yet burnes his wings. . . . [28]

Moreover, when he speaks, in one place, of a marigold that opens to the sun though it have no tongue to say so,[29] and in another place of

> A Pregnant banke swel'd up, to rest
> The violets reclining head,[30]

he strikes a note—particularly in the latter—so distinctly in a poetic tradition alien to him that one is surprised and puzzled.

In a more familiar vein are such figures as that in which he describes how he had sought to escape detection by his mistress' father:

> I taught my silkes, their whistling to forbeare,
> Even my opprest shoes, dumbe and speechlesse
> were;

but how, nevertheless, he was betrayed by

> A loud perfume, which at my entrance cryed
> Even at thy fathers nose, so were wee spied.[31]

Personifications slight in extent but powerful in suggestion are that sudden outcry in "The First Anniversary"— "How witty's ruine!" [32] and its kin in "The Expostulation"—

> In plaguing him, let misery be witty.[33]

They are brief and abrupt, but they leave circles of ripples spreading out in the reader's imagination.

In several other of these personifications the accent is on bodily infirmities: thus winter is seen as the "decrepit time," [34] a lone groat looks lean and threadbare,[35] a poem is lame and weak,[36] watching-candles are thin, wretched and sick,[37] and in "Loves Diet," bemoaning a love beyond control, he writes:

> To what a cumbersome unwieldinesse

And burdenous corpulence my love had growne,
But that I did, to make it lesse,
And keepe it in proportion,
Give it a diet, made it feed upon
That which love worst endures, discretion.[38]

Another small group of figures finds in the human body rather elaborate parallels to the organization of society, and thus presents the reverse, as it were, of those images which found parallels to man's body, the microcosm, in the macrocosm of the universe. The world is a man, he declares in Satyre V,

in which, officers
Are the devouring stomache, and Suiters
The excrements. . . .[39]

and that world contains, he says in "A Funerall Elegie,"

Princes for armes, and Councellors for braines,
Lawyers for tongues, Divines for hearts, and more,
The Rich for stomackes, and for backes, the
Poore;
The Officers for hands, Merchants for feet.[40]

Similar figures appear in Meditation 12 and Satyre I: in the former he takes the phrase "body politic" literally and points out that the king is its heart, the council its brain, magistrates its sinews which tie all together, rumor and calumny its infectious and deadly vapour-sickness;[41] and in the latter he describes those statesmen

which teach how to tie
The sinewes of a cities mistique bodie.[42]

The only other parts of the body that occur repeatedly are the eyes, but for the most part they do so only in conventional metaphors suggestive of no positive feeling or special observation. All in all, there is little evidence among these

personifications of interest in the body in action, the myriad expressions of the human face or any of those numerous less obvious aspects of man's behaviour that provided
Shakespeare with many of the most brilliant and memorable of his images.

BIRTH AND DEATH

The last group to be dealt with is the imagery from
man's spiritual attributes and natural functions. Here we
find metaphors from the soul, sleep, dreams, love relations,
birth and death, but since the images from all except the
last of these are sparse, merely allusive, and generally
unimpressive, it is on those from birth and death that we
must concentrate. It may, however, be pointed out in
passing that the paucity of images from love and love
relations is perhaps misleading evidence. Love is the actual subject of much of Donne's verse and, as was the
case with religious figures, we find that where it is the
subject he avoids using it as a source of illustration or
analogy. The handful of images which he does draw from
love appears in his religious verse; in the chapter on
"Religion and the Bible" we observed how these contributed their share to that tendency of Donne's to mingle the
erotic and the divine.

On turning to the images from birth, death and all the
circumstances attending both we find that they form an
extraordinarily large group and one of the most interesting in Donne. There is, however, no balance between the
two extremes, for it is plain at once that his figures from
man's death, burial and disintegration completely out-
weigh the sprinkling drawn from the circumstances that
surround his birth. The obsessive preoccupation of the
entire seventeenth century with the idea of death needs no

introduction. If death itself is not the theme, its shadowy influence is cast over almost every major writing of the time, ranging in substance from the sense of man's mortality, life's brevity and the swift ruin of beauty in writers like Shakespeare, Raleigh, and, later, Sir Thomas Browne, to the almost pathological interest in the decay of the flesh and the horrors of the grave in the sermons of most preachers and in the plays of the Websters and the Fords.

Donne turns to both phases, sometimes ruminating on the transiency of earthly things, but more frequently pulling away the shroud and dwelling with morbid fervor on the gruesome work of the worm. Compared with death, birth is but a minor phenomenon. In fact, with the perverse logic of morbidity, Donne sees birth as only the entrance to death, the beginning of the end—the very act which makes decay possible. "We have a winding-sheet in our mothers womb," he says in his last and greatest sermon, *Death's Duell,* "that grows with us from our conception, and we come into the world wound up in that winding-sheet; for we come to seek a grave. . . ."[43] And conversely, of course, death is a birth—a beginning, for some, of immortal life.

Donne's images from death are drawn not only from the essential spiritual concept, but from all the physical accompaniments, from—to list only the more important— prayers, passing bell, carcass, embalming, coffin, dead-cart, grave, tomb, urn, epitaph, worm, and death's-head. But very few of this great number—there are well over four score—go beyond the simplest type of metaphor. The majority are such elementary figures as those which refer to the year's end as a death, to the sickbed as a grave, to the world as a grave-yard, and to human parasites as devouring worms.

Of those which do go further, several cluster around

the death of a virtuous man, and particularly the serene way in which such a man dies. The most interesting of these is contained in those lines in "A Valediction: forbidding mourning" in which Donne, advising his beloved wife just how quiet should be the temporary parting between them, says:

> As virtuous men passe mildly away,
>   And whisper to their soules, to goe,
> Whilst some of their sad friends doe say,
>   The breath goes now, and some say, no:
>
> So let us melt, and make no noise.[44]

Thus, to illustrate how undemonstrative he and his wife should be in parting, he chooses, of all things, a deathbed scene, and, passing over its most characteristic aspects, pitches upon the peacefulness with which one man passes away. It is an excellent example of the unexpected, though not therefore unfamiliar places in which Donne finds images, and, in addition, of that obliquity by which he uses the least obvious phase of that to which he has turned. How very close to actual experience this image was is made vividly clear by a personal note in the sermon preached at the funeral of Sir William Cokayne: " . . . his last and dying words," Donne testified, "were the repetition of the name of Jesus; and when he had not strength to utter that name, distinctly and perfectly, they might hear it from within him, as from a man afar off. . . ."[45] Moreover, he seems to have much the same kind of scene in mind when he describes the affectionate letters sent by friends to Sir Henry Wotton as coming thickly—

> as prayers ascend
> To heaven in troupes at'a good mans passing
>   bell;[46]

and in still another when he suggests, in a mood typical of his epithalamia, that the bride's celerity in retiring should be such that before any one can even say goodnight she

> Should vanish from her cloathes, into her bed,
> As Soules from bodies steale, and are not spy'd.[47]

This is but one of a surprising number of images wherein an aspect of death is used, usually grotesquely, to illustrate some phase of lovers' relations. Love itself is a death, says Donne, and no man can even assert he has loved,

> for who can say
> Hee was kill'd yesterday? [48]

Thus, too, the bridal bed becomes "virginity's grave"; [49] and a bride waiting in bed is compared to a faithful man ready to give his life for the sake of another.[50] Although, on the one hand, despondency resulting from love is a grave,[51] and absence between lovers makes them carcasses,[52] woman possessed is only mummy.[53] This is absurdly paradoxical—but paradox is after all the very essence of Donne's general attitude where love and women are concerned.

It is of course to be expected that such a subject as death should supply a good many examples of the fantastic, and also of that extravagance for which Donne has frequently been criticized. These range from such repulsive figures as that of the soul as a worm on the world's carcass, beauty's wrinkles as love's graves, the faces of the aged as death's-heads, cities as sepulchres in which dwell carcasses, his library as his coffin, and of a friend's absence as rendering London a carcass poorly embalmed with meagre amusements, to such merely fanciful ones as

> . . . a Lute, which in moist weather, rings
> Her knell alone, by cracking of her strings.[54]

Several make use of violent and sudden death: in one he compares the movements of the world after Elizabeth Drury's passing with those of a beheaded man; though the blood spout from his trunk and head, Donne reports,

> His eyes will twinckle, and his tongue will roll,
> As though he beckned, and cal'd backe his soule,
> He graspes his hands, and he pulls up his feet,
> And seemes to reach, and to step forth to meet
> His soule. . . .[55]

and in another he draws a parallel between one who whispers treason to another and thus involves him, and a man who wounds with a stiletto of gold, strangles with scarfs of silk, smothers with down of phoenixes, or stifles with a perfume of amber [56]—an exotic, not to say outlandish series apparently fabricated to fit the need. A figure almost as bizarre, but one which makes appropriate as well as effective use of graveyard machinery, comes from that image-laden verse letter, "The Storme," and pictures seasick voyagers caught in a storm:

> Some coffin'd in their cabbins lye, 'equally
> Griev'd that they are not dead, and yet must dye;
> And as sin-burd'ned soules from graves will
>   creepe,
> At the last day, some forth their cabbins peepe:
> And tremblingly'aske what newes. . . .[57]

Equally fantastic but a perfect symbol of mocking futility is the image that occurs to Donne when he threatens to die as revenge on his unfeeling mistress; then, he says to her, your beauties will be as worthless as unmined gold,

> And all your graces no more use shall have
>   Then a Sun dyall in a grave.[58]

In the process of birth Donne seems to find no parallel mysteries; it awakens no comparable awe and little specu-

lation. The swaddling, teething and weaning of children
are mentioned, as are cradles, midwife, and womb, but all
play a negligible part. Pregnancy, figuring vividly in a few
passages, comes closest to being an exception. Writing to
Edward Gilpin, probably during the plague, he declares
that London is without pleasures, that theatres are empty,
and as

> lancke and thin is every street and way
> As a woman deliver'd yesterday.[59]

In Satyre IIII, plagued by a garrulous courtier, Donne
sighs and sweats, ready to travail—like "a bigge wife, at
sight of loathed meat"; [60] and in time of sickness, exas-
perated by his own impatience at the slow maturing of his
illness, he exclaims:

> A woman that is weake cannot put off her ninth
> moneth to a tenth . . . and say shee will stay till
> shee bee stronger; nor a Queene cannot hasten it to
> a seventh, that shee may bee ready for some other
> pleasure.[61]

But as ready as he is to use such reasonable notions of
birth, so ready is he to use popular tales and vulgar
errors. To his purpose are such fabulous stories of methods
of generation as that of creatures which hatch their eggs
simply by looking at them, of snakes alleged to rise from
dung, and of the nameless things popularly supposed to
issue mysteriously from the mud of old Nile.[62] Because
he used them without indicating his own opinion, it is difficult to decide whether he actually believed these tales or
utilized them only because they were to his purpose. We
may give him the benefit of the doubt and say that he
knew the difference, but it is well to remember that many
Elizabethans as acute and discerning as Donne were still
ready to give not a few such conceptions their *imprimatur*.

THE EVIDENCE

PART III

XVII

NATURE

Among the considerable variety of major themes in Elizabethan-Jacobean literature, nature is definitely unimportant; the contemplation of flowers and trees and landscapes for their own sake is rare and is confined for the most part to minor poems replete with classical echoes. But, although it was not until Thomson, Burns and the writers of the Romantic period that the poetic possibilities of nature were really explored, it had always of course been a conventional source of imagery, embellishment and incidental effects. As such, it played a prominent part in the verse of Sidney, Lodge, Breton, and Spenser, and in pastoral poetry in general; and we have observed, especially in our study of his avoidance of images from mythology, how vigorously Donne rebelled against this tradition. His reaction to imagery from aspects of nature reinforces this evidence clearly and conclusively.

That Donne thought consciously of nature as a too common source of poetic imagery and that he was repelled by the triteness and exhaustion of meaning that had come from over-use, he makes evident more than once. In a verse letter written to the Countess of Salisbury, one of his many patronesses, he says:

> the Sunne
> Growne stale, is to so low a value runne,
> That his disshevel'd beames and scattered fires
> Serve but for Ladies Periwigs and Tyres
> In lovers Sonnets.[1]

He knows, too, the conventional symbols from nature and
therefore his avoidance of them must be construed as other
than accidental. In fact, he makes a sophisticated lover
use these ironically and say to his mistress:

> Thou art not soft, and cleare, and strait, and
>   faire,
> As Down, as Stars, Cedars, and Lillies are,
> But thy right hand, and cheek, and eye, only
> Are like thy other hand, and cheek, and eye.[2] *

What is surprising, then, is the fact that all in all Donne
has as many images from nature as he has. His biography
reveals no such associations with nature or country life
as, for example, we find in the case of Herrick; from the
Jack Donne of his youth to the Dean Donne of his later
years, his name is almost always associated with London
and city life. The answer seems to be that he was hardly
conscious of the number of his allusions in this direction.
Few of them are elaborate or strained; few are startling;
the great majority are of the casual or incidental type
that make up the bulk of any poet's images.

He notes, it is true, the fundamental aspects of growth
—the fecundity of earth, the quickening of life in the
spring, the awakening of roots and the blossoming that
follows; but there is little of that care and interest which
gives new vitality to fading figures. His heart was not
here. If during the hectic days of his youth or his later
life as preacher he paused occasionally to wander through
field or garden, he chose, when he sat down to write, to
use very little of what he had observed, and then only the
simplest elements. Ill and getting on in years, he writes,
". . . I should as soon look for Roses at this time of the
year, as look for increase of strength;"[3] elsewhere, the

---

* For a comparable attitude see Shakespeare's Sonnet 130.

soul that, thankful for every blessing, turns to God, is a
dilating flower at sunrise; when, at some blasphemy, that
soul gathers in as though stricken, it is a flower contract-
ing at sunset.[4] In other images he utilizes the helplessness
of flowers floating on water or caught in a whirlpool, the
new strength and color of a transplanted violet, the clasp
of ivy, the number of the primrose's petals, weeds and
thorns, the sapless leaf, and the stick which supports the
precious plant but does not feed it.

When one of these images, simple as it may be, does
occur in the middle of a typical sermon filled with typical
seventeenth century biblical exegesis, it is as startling to
the modern reader as any lone flower in a field of dry
stalks. In such an expanse of prose appears the comparison of the atheist who sees God but has not the grace to
confess it with the marigold which "opens to the sun,
though it have no tongue to say so." [5] Once, however, for
the sake of a patroness, he takes flowers and wreathes them
into a tribute fantastic with involutions. Speaking of the
court with all its female pensioners, he says to Lady
Bedford:

> 'Tis but a grave of spices, till your face
> Exhale them, and a thick close bud display.
>   Widow'd and reclus'd else, her sweets
>   she'enshrines;
> As China, when the Sunne at Brasill dines,[6]

thus evolving as conceited a compliment as any Elizabethan gentlewoman could desire.

But perhaps the most impressive of Donne's images
from flowers is that which comes from the simple act of
gathering them. Seeking to carry his auditory into an
O altitudo of religious speculation concerning the length of
a day in heaven, he cried out:

> Methusalem, with all his hundreds of years, was
> but a mushroom of a night's growth, to this day,
> and all the four monarchies, with all their thou-
> sands of years, and all the powerful kings, and all
> the beautiful queens of this world, were but as a bed
> of flowers, some gathered at six, some at seven, some
> at eight, all in one morning, in respect of this day.[7]

Although a mushroom of a night's growth as symbol of the
brevity of man's life is vivid, it is overshadowed by the
extraordinary analogy between the span of all the monarchs of history and flowers plucked in the early morning
of a single day.

So bizarre that they may be said to issue more from
fanciful rumor and folktalk than any reality of nature are
the images drawn from the stories surrounding the mandrake. With at least half a dozen grotesque characteristics to choose from, Donne found these strange plants
useful again and again. Epitomizing the impossible in his
famous "Goe, and catche a falling starre," he exclaimed,

> Get with child a mandrake root; [8]

describing the world after Prince Henry's death:

> such a life we have,
> As but so many mandrakes on his grave; [9]

and bemoaning his faithless mistress:

> Make me a mandrake, so I may groane here,[10]

using in turn the plant's fancied resemblance to a human
being, its reputed tendency to grow on graves and to groan
when uprooted.

Although almost as infrequent as those from flowers,
Donne's images from trees seem to reveal somewhat more
than a layman's interest. Typical of the sources he uses

in this group are winter sap flowing to the root, grafting, shaking trees to secure fruit, a worm-eaten trunk, and gangrened limbs that drop through their own weight or turbulency. Specific trees are brought into the picture when in Elegie VIII, comparing the arms of his mistress with those of another's mistress, he calls the former slender stalks whose ends are quivering woodbine, and those of the latter just rough-barked elm-boughs.[11] To describe a trembling woman he uses the conventional figure of the aspen,[12] but speaking of his own letters, he writes to Sir Henry Goodere:

> This much information is in very leaves, that they can tell what the tree is. . . . Of what generall use, the fruit should speake, and I have none . . . yet even of barren Sycamores, such as I, there were use, if either any light flashings, or scorching vehemencies, or sudden showres made you need so shadowy an example or remembrancer.[13]

Rare is the rural simplicity of the figure in which a great man's death is said to leave each of those who leaned on him, like sweet briars deprived of the tree which supported them;[14] and just as rare is such an image as that in Meditation 19 where Donne really ventures into parallels from the fine art of tree tendance; in it the slow progress of his illness calls to mind the patience and care that all nature demands:

> . . . some tree beares no fruit, except much dung be laid about it . . . some trees require much visiting, must watring, much labour . . . some trees require incision, and pruning, and lopping . . . some trees require the early and the often accesse of the Sunne . . . some trees must be housd and

kept within doores. . . . As Nature will not, so
power and greatnesse will not bee put to change
their seasons; and shall wee looke for this Indul-
gence in a disease, or thinke to shake it off before it
bee ripe? [15]

It goes far enough to suggest that his limited use of trees
is no certain indication of lack of knowledge.

* *

Donne's images from nature as cultivated by man, from
farm and orchard and vineyard, that is, are no more
numerous or remarkable than those from trees. Donne
certainly did not avoid the so-called unpoetic as a source
of imagery but the realism which could make full use in
verse of even the drabbest aspects of farm life was part of
an esthetic undreamed of in 1595. It is in truth remarkable that Donne used as many and as realistic figures from
this source as he did. Perhaps noteworthy is the fact that
the majority of these images from farming—approximately
twenty-five out of forty—appear in the prose and are for
the most part prosaic and, so to speak, earth-bound.

Although farming is used so sparingly, the emphasis,
in those figures that do appear, seems in general to be on
the less pleasant aspects of life on the land—the stubborn-
ness of stony ground, plowed fields choked with weed, good
seed straggling into cockle, harvests nipped in the bud,
tender fruit devoured by caterpillars, thorns and weeds
. . . weeds and thorns. . . . The attractive side of the
picture, seed multiplying, corn ripening on the ear, reap-
ing, gleaning, the golden harvest, appears all too infrequently. Definitely of the former group, and an analogy
which Donne explores perhaps more thoroughly than any
other in his prose, is the powerful seventy-line figure in
the *Devotions,* which begins:

How ruinous a farme hath man taken, in taking himselfe? How ready is the house every day to fall downe, and how is all the ground overspread with weeds, all the body with diseases? where not onely every turfe, but every stone, beares weeds . . . every little flint upon the face of this soile, hath some infectious weede. . . . How deare, and how often a rent doth Man pay for this farme? hee paies twice a day, in double meales, and how little time he hath to raise his rent? How many holy daies to call him from his labour?

and ends:

When therefore I tooke this farme, undertooke this body, I undertooke to draine, not a marish, but a moat, where there was, not water mingled to offend, but all was water; I undertooke to perfume dung, where no one part, but all was equally unsavory. . . . To cure the sharpe accidents of diseases, is a great worke . . . but to cure the body, the root . . . is a worke reserved for the great Phisitian. . . .[16]

This is a typical prose image in its straightforward clarity, its shunning of ellipsis or poetic condensation, and even in that repetitiousness by which it attains emphasis and cumulative impact. This and another in which he refers to David's understanding and care of his conscience in terms of husbanding and manuring, and of knowing what plowing, harrowing, weeding, watering, and pruning it needed,[17] are exceptional in the thoroughness of their reference to farm practice. A minor parallel, but one which occurs often enough to suggest that the association is remarkably strong in the poet's mind is that of the act of love as tilling and woman as arable earth [18]—a natural paradise if the woman is the poet's beloved,[19] stony ground if she is someone else's,[20] and public land if she is free to many.[21]

Vivid as a few of these images may be, the group as a whole is obviously unimpressive. It suggests little personal acquaintance with the type of life touched on; what acquaintance it does show may remind us perhaps that books on husbandry—including some in verse—were among the most widely circulated of the time, and that Donne glancing through such volumes would be more in his element than Donne wandering among the cows, the sheep, and the dandelions.

XVIII

THE HEAVENS

In the chapter on "Ideas of the Universe" we considered the large group of figures drawn from theories in astronomy and cosmology; we come now to those which seem to issue directly or indirectly from sensory experience of the natural phenomena of the heavens. Here we find Donne drawing imagery from many aspects of the skies, from the sense of the limiting curtain of the firmament, and of the earth as a ball beneath it, from the winds and the clouds, thunder and lightning and rain, from moon and stars and, most of all, from the sun—from the sun and its denial, shadow.

The cosmic point of view, wherein the writer soars until the earth beneath seems but a globe in space, comes but rarely in Donne. Even those images in which he envisions man as a little world, microcosm to that macrocosm which is the universe, are, as we have seen, part of an ancient theory, later integral to the Paracelsian system, and therefore really bookish in origin. Occasionally, however, Donne fits into this traditional parallel, analogies which seem to be drawn from his own reactions to the surrounding world. Thus, if man is a little world, then a sick man is one who "hath these earthquakes in him selfe, sodaine shakings; these lightnings, sodaine flashes; these thunders, sodaine noises; these Eclypses, sodain offuscations," [1] and so on; and in another he finds man a veritable planet, with blood-vessels rivers, sinews veins of mines, muscles hills, bones stone quarries, until the "Aire would be too litle for this Orbe of Man to move in, the firmament would bee but enough for this Starre. . . ." [2]

Occasionally he takes a position—somewhere between heaven and earth—from which he can observe not only the firmament above but also the broadest aspects of the world beneath. In the result, which might be called the topography of Donne's verse, a pair of lovers become two hemispheres; the country a desert; sickness a bog; and truth a huge hill, cragged and steep.[3] Completing the topographical map is death as another desert—the greatest, of course,—until the funeral service of a patron, when, in the exaggerated language of patron-service, it is at once metaphorically transformed into the paradise of a royal court.[4]

But these, though broad, are earthly vistas. Above is the sun—at one time or another symbol of God, a patroness, the poet's mistress, a woman's hair or eyes, the king, or the unfolded mysteries of knowledge—all this though he had, as we have seen, recognized the triteness of the sun as image source. Beclouding and dampening as symbols of misfortune, and his beloved's eyes as lightning are almost as conventional; hardly less so are the hateful Flavia's face as a cloud turning day to night;[5] the bride's coming as the sunrising;[6] and finally the bride who has mercy on beholders and bedecks herself, as the sun beclouded or reflected in water.[7]

If we exclude definitely astronomical images, the night sky yields little for Donne. Endymion, Artemis, Silene and most of the other romantic moon legends popular with Elizabethan sonneteers are in Donne conspicuous by their absence. Once he hazards the metaphor of the moon as symbol of the changeable though permanent;[8] in another place thoughts as stars of the soul;[9] and in a third, how the glory of the next world can be seen best from the depths of calamity is illustrated by the curious fact that stars can be seen better from the bottom of a well than from a high steeple.[10] What happened, however, when Donne applied himself to the type of conceit made famous by the sonneteers is exemplified by the following, wherein a bride's eyes bring up not only stars but also birth and farming:

> Then from these wombes of starres, the Brides
> bright eyes,
> At every glance, a constellation flyes,
> And sowes the Court with starres, and doth
> prevent
> In light and power, the all-ey'd firmament.[11]

It is interesting to note that this is one of the figures which Samuel Johnson used in his life of Cowley to illustrate the so-called "metaphysical" conceit. Considering the ornate artificiality of the figure, it is not hard to understand why Johnson could introduce it with the words, "Their thoughts and expressions were sometimes grossly absurd, and such as no figures or licence can reconcile to the understanding," but it is very significant concerning his entire approach to Donne that he chose to deal with one of the most affected of the poet's images as if it were typical.

Shadow, the positive sign of light denied, fascinated Donne. And of the images which explore the symbolism of shadows, by far the most elaborate is that which makes up the poem called "A Lecture upon the Shadow." The twenty-six lines of this piece present parallels between the progress of love and the shadows of lovers who walk in the sun—a series of images as typical in their ellipses, intertwining and precision as any in the poet's work. We can distinguish such juxtapositions as that between the disguises adopted by beginning love and morning shadows; between the casting away of these disguises in the maturity of such love and the shadowlessness of high noon; between disguises resumed and ever increased by lovers in the decline of true love, and the new shadows, ever-lengthening, after high noon. The final couplet,

> Love is a growing, or full constant light;
> And his first minute, after noone, is night,

caps a series of paradoxical interpretations with a complete distortion of the image idea, the course of the sun, to fit the development of the major idea, love. This progression of shadow, changing throughout the day, attracted Donne's attention again and again. We have seen with what care he uses it in a familiar poem; not so familiar, but as meticulous in detail, is the prose passage wherein he identifies unpleasant implications in a text with those same morning shadows. The implications are eliminated before the end of the first part of the text as are shadows when the sun reaches its meridional height; the reappearance of the difficulties in the second part of the text, and, finally, their overwhelming the reader, are afternoon shadows which lengthen into night.[12] It is interesting to note how little difference there is between the material, or the way it is used, in the two media.

In one image in "The First Anniversary" modern man compared with ancient man is said to be less than his "Fathers shadowes cast at noone";[13] and in Elegie XIX a woman disrobing, Donne says,

> such beautious state reveals,
> As when from flowry meads th'hills shadow
> steales.[14]

But the two images which carry this interest in shadow almost into the realm of fantasy are that of the height of futility seen as a man who races his own shadow,[15] and of the cheated wretch who sues at law as

> . . . the swimming dog whom shadows cosened,
> And div'st, neare drowning, for what's vanished.[16]

It is, however, in a friendly letter—where one would hardly
expect such meticulousness or literary formality—that we
find an image which contains, in epitome, a treatise on the
nature of shadow. Donne has pictured his friend Goodere
as living in the sun of the royal court while he himself, in
the country, is far removed from its heat; it is, nevertheless, no darkness which he dwells in but that very different
thing, shadow,

> which is not no light, but a pallid, waterish, and
> diluted one. As all shadows are of one colour, if
> you respect the body from which they are cast (for
> our shadows upon clay will be dirty, and in a garden
> green, and flowery) so all retirings into a shadowy
> life are alike from all causes, and alike subject to
> the barbarousness and insipid dulnesse of the
> Country; onely the emploiment, and that upon
> which you cast and bestow your pleasure, businesse,
> or books, gives it the tincture, and beauty.[17]

*   *

The sense of the time of day or the season of the year,
although only scantily revealed in a handful of metaphors
from dawn, twilight, day, night, and the four seasons,
deserves a moment's attention here.

Youth and age are figured in the contrast, on the one
hand, between spring and autumn or winter, and, on the
other, between morning and twilight; youth's wantonness, in the first heats of day; and the death which closes
all, in the darkness of darkest night. This is fairly conventional; the entire sequence becomes Donne's own, however,
in such a laconic pair of lines as he addressed to Sir Henry
Goodere:

> So had your body'her morning, hath her noone,
> And shall not better; her next change is
> night.[18]

Outside this traditional if vivid pattern wherein youth is morning or spring and old age night or winter stands the much quoted tribute to Magdalen Herbert:

> No Spring, nor Summer Beauty hath such grace,
> As I have seen in one Autumnall face.[19]

The tenderness and nostalgia of this image—qualities rare in Donne—were evoked here by beauty growing mellow with age; compare it with the more familiar Donnean attitude called forth by age which has brought ugliness:

> But name not Winter-faces, whose skin's slacke;
> Lanke, as an unthrifts purse. . . .[20]

There is, in addition, an image which refers to the middle years as the summer of life;[21] it adds the completing touch to this pattern of associations. However, the kind of paradox that conceits tend to weave appears in the contrast between one image of lovers' hours as eternities,[22] and another of love itself as but a summer's night. The latter is embedded in a passage whose melody might well cause regret that Donne wooed ruggedness so consistently:

> So, lovers dreame a rich and long delight,
> But get a winter-seeming summers night.[23]

Of all nights, St. Lucy's, longest in the year, seems to have intrigued him most. It became the subject of his "A Nocturnall upon S. Lucies Day," and, in imagery, the symbol of death's duration—longest of nights to men, a mere night to eternal life hereafter.[24] Death without the prospect of such resurrection is, he suggests in one of his sermons, winter everlasting.[25]

XIX

RIVERS AND SEAS

All that was said by way of introduction to the chapter
on "Sea Travel and Exploration" concerning Donne's acquaintance with travel by water might well be repeated
here as background for a brief consideration of the images
he takes from streams, rivers and seas themselves. It must
be said that the knowledge of these things which Donne
does display is in no way so technical or complex that it
might not have been attained through casual contacts.
Although there is much in these images that suggests real
interest, there is all in all little in Donne of that attraction to the sea as symbol of the mysterious, to the play of
light on water, or to the infinite patterns of current and
eddy, that has distinguished the work of many poets.

The most elaborate figure in this group, running
through two pages of prose, pictures the world as a sea.
Disturbances are tempests, he says; changes in men's
bodies and minds are ebbs and floods; and purposes beyond
understanding, waters bottomless to sounding lines. Convenient but not really satisfying, this world is like sea-
water which quenches no thirst, and as the world is only
a stopping place, so the sea is only a place of passage. In
both, the great devour the smaller, and, finally, a man
spending some thought on this world and some on heaven
is like a ship partly below water, partly above.[1] The
sense one gets from such a figure of the sea as a place of
danger and difficulty is borne out by image after image.
Nor is it hard to understand why an Elizabethan traveller,
knowing only sail-driven vessels, should look upon the

sea, with its winds and storms, its unimaginable vastness and insatiable appetite, and its fantastic denizens, as the epitome of such things as misery, sin, and death.

In illness Donne's afflictions are a sea, too deep for him, in which a ship is the only physician.[2] Elsewhere he visualizes this life as only a narrow bridge on which we stand, "giddy" and "vertiginous," over the "deep and roaring waters, and desperate whirlpools as this world abounds with." [3] Of his mother's life he wrote that it was a sea under continual tempest, a life in which the way had been "strait, stormie, obscure." [4] A number of images identify the sea, naturally enough, with the last and greatest of afflictions, death; several of these come vividly to life. Man is the world, he says in his elegy on Lady Marckham, but death is an ocean which environs all,

> and though as yet
> God hath set markes, and bounds, twixt us
> and it,
> Yet doth it rore, and gnaw, and still pretend,
> And breaks our bankes, when ere it takes a
> friend.[5]

But there is a consolation in the belief that death when it takes the body, frees the soul, as "the sea, when it gaines, loseth too." [6] In fact, in the case of such a one as he writes of here, exception must be made to all ominous associations, for death's effect on her—far from being degrading —is a wonderfully delicate enhancement; in her

> this sea of death hath made no breach,
> But as the tide doth wash the slimie beach,
> And leaves embroder'd workes upon the sand,
> So is her flesh refin'd by deaths cold hand,[7]

an image which in its grave beauty and sombre music recalls sharply more than one passage in Shakespeare's sonnets. In these qualities it is not equalled even by those lines in "A Hymne to God the Father" when, envisioning the sea of death, he confesses:

> I have a sinne of feare, that when I have spunne
> My last thred, I shall perish on the shore.[8]

* *

Sporadically, and rarely in any detail, Donne utilizes in his imagery various phenomena of river and stream: the brackish taste which sweet water acquires as it approaches the sea, the circling of eddies, silt brought down by swollen waters, the new channels made by thwarted streams, and meadows inundated by flood; but what catches his eye most often is a floating thing at the mercy of moving water. Thus men who turn from trusting God to trusting those who unjustly claim power from him are like flowers that thrive at the rough stream's calm head until, having given themselves to its rage, they are driven

> Through mills, and rockes, and woods, and at
> last, almost
> Consum'd in going, in the sea are lost.[9]

Similarly, a man who sets his heart on riches, beauty or honor—the transitory things of life—is like one who has cast a paper into a river and bound his eye to the impossible task of following it;[10] and he who loves a fickle woman is a floating flower caught in a whirlpool.[11] In this last image Donne berates his mistress for her inconstancy; on the other hand, in Elegie XVII, significantly called "Variety," he perversely calls the very same characteristic his own ideal, pointing out that rivers which run "wide and farr" are clear and pleasing while

> a dead lake that no strange bark doth greet
> Corrupts it self and what doth live in it.[12]

In the first of these two figures he laments inconstancy—
in someone else; if there is any doubt as to what he pre-
scribed for himself—in poetry if not in reality—the following blunt image settles the matter most emphatically:

> Waters stincke soone, if in one place they bide,
> And in the vast sea are more putrifi'd;
> But when they kisse one banke, and leaving this
> Never looke backe, but the next banke doe kisse,
> Then are they purest.[13]

Apparently, however, it is not loveless promiscuity he de-
sires as much as occasional change, for change, he observes in the next couplet, is the nursery of "musicke, joy,
life, and eternity." Donne seems to have associated such
irregular relationships between men and women with the
varying movement of streams, for Elegie VI presents us
with still another parallel of this kind, this time of wife
as stream and husband as channel. It continues for four-
teen lines, but I quote it in its entirety as an unusual
example in Donne of a passage which in many respects—
its idyllic atmosphere, its occasional melodiousness, the
quality of its conceits, and certain touches of poetic diction—is surprisingly Spenserian:

> When I behold a streame, which, from the spring,
> Doth with a doubtfull melodious murmuring,
> Or in a speechlesse slumber, calmely ride
> Her wedded channels bosome, and then chide
> And bend her browes, and swell if any bough
> Do but stoop downe, or kisse her upmost brow;
> Yet, if her often gnawing kisses winne
> The traiterous banke to gape, and let her in,
> She rusheth violently, and doth divorce
> Her from her native, and her long-kept course,
> And rores, and braves it, and in a gallant scorne,

> In flattering eddies promising retorne,
> She flouts the channell, who thenceforth is drie;
> Then say I; that is shee, and this am I." [14]

The last line, abrupt and vigorous, offers refreshing contrast to the lush alliteration and onomatopoeia of the first six lines, and to such conceits as "channels bosome," "gnawing kisses," and "traiterous banke."

Another association, appearing in a pair of images in Satyre V, is based on a conception of judges, or high officers of courts, as treacherous and corrupt. In lines 14-16 he introduces them as

> vast ravishing seas; and Suiters,
> Springs; now full, now shallow, now drye,
> which, to
> That which drownes them, run— [15]

a prelude to that dramatic declaration in lines 45 and following that here there can be no appeal, for the power of the lower courts flows

> from the first maine head, and these can
> throw
> Thee, if they sucke thee in, to misery,
> To fetters, halters;

and that if you dare to complain

> thou go'st
> Against the stream, when upwards: when thou
> art most
> Heavy and most faint;

only to find that those against whom you are complaining are become

> great seas, o'r which, when thou shalt bee
> Forc'd to make golden bridges, thou shalt see
> That all thy gold was drown'd in them before.

Thus are the sundry, almost random difficulties which
Donne associated with river and sea combined to provide
a dark picture of the judicial process; it confirms what
we have already learned concerning Donne's attitude toward Elizabethan courts of law, but it does not alter our
feeling that he was only moderately sensitive to the sub-
tler aspects and the changing beauties of English river
and stream.

XX

ANIMALS—REAL AND FABULOUS

More a student of books than of nature itself, Donne in his images from animal life may be expected to reflect the reigning tradition in natural history as much as any actual observation. A glance at such books as Edward Topsell's *The Historie of Four-footed Beasts and Serpents* (1607), John Maplet's *A Greene Forest, or a Naturall Historie* (1567), or, perhaps more significant than these, a literary work like Lyly's *Euphues,* shows just how popular the unnatural natural history of the elder Pliny and of Aristotle still was. The most incredibility fantastic tales concerning real animals as well as entirely non-existent creatures were everywhere prevalent, and even a Sir Thomas Browne, as late as 1646, bringing some scientific training and not a little skepticism to bear, could puncture only the most outlandish of these.

Several images do suggest that Donne, like many Elizabethans, probably did have some experience with those animals or birds which were used in popular sports—with stag, dog, hawk, and game bird—those, in fact, that we have already dealt with in connection with the sports of which they are an essential part.*

Of the animals symbols from the Bible only a few—and these the most familiar—appear: the serpent standing for wiliness, the dove for mildness, and the lamb for Christ.[1]

In addition, there are, almost as a matter of course, the conventional metaphors alluding to the lechery of the goat, the cunning of the fox, the mimicry of the ape, the kingly

---

* See chapter on "Sports and Games."

eminence of the lion, the tamed nature of the broken colt, the grovelling of worms, the slowness of snails, and the untrustworthiness of beasts in general. These are so commonplace as to be used almost without thought concerning the creatures actually referred to; in fact, we might almost as validly have dealt with them among the literary figures in our consideration of images from the arts. More elaborate but hardly less conventional is the metaphor of the world as a beehive;[2] or bees as symbols of a diligence whose result is honey.[3] The polity of ants suggests a similar parallel; cities are ant-hills, Donne says,

> Where, when the severall labourers I see,
> For children, house, Provision, taking paine,
> They'are all but Ants, carrying eggs, straw,
>   and grain.[4]

Of other small creatures the worm finds a place in many figures as symbol not only of that which grovels but also of corruption[5] and of parasitical human beings.[6] The snail, besides being "slow-paced," has the unique distinction of naturally carrying his home with him; imitate him, Donne exhorts Sir Henry Wotton, dwell in thyself—

> Bee thine owne Palace, or the world's thy gaile.[7]

Flatterers, attractive but producing nothing, and heretics who build up ineffectual churches are likened to wasps who make honeyless combs;[8] Jesuits are described as caterpillars which devour the tender fruit;[9] and in Elegie VI a lover is a "giddie flie" which gets its wings burnt in the flame of a mistress.[10] The spider is another source of such metaphors: Love, Donne observes in "Twicknam Garden," is like a spinning spider, for it

> transubstantiates all,
> And can convert Manna to gall;[11]

statesmen who use vice against vice are like those who use toads against spiders;[12] and over-refined interpretations have made Scriptures, which are "strong toils to . . . destroy the boar and bear which devast our Lord's vineyard," into "fine cobwebs to catch flies" and have changed strong cables into threads of silkworms.[13]

If we pass over references to those birds obviously a part of such pursuits as falconry and hawking (and therefore already dealt with elsewhere), only a scattering of images remains. There are allusions to death as a bird of prey, to a watchman as an owl, to a sinner as an eagle in ambitions, and to sharp-tongued Julia as a

> night-crow, whose ill boding cries
> Give out for nothing but new injuries.[14]

Only in two passages does he think of the caged bird: the way preachers change at court reminds him of such birds forgetting native notes as they learn new ones;[15] and in Probleme XVIII a man writing history in prison—as Raleigh did—suggests the way a bird in a cage takes its tune from each passing whistler.[16] Angling excepted, the metaphors from water creatures are equally meagre. We have a commonplace reference to the pike which devours lesser fish, and several unimportant ones to those curious creatures, the clinging, sucker-like remora and the torpedo fish with its electric rays. An image that really warrants attention occurs in the Heroical Epistle, "Sapho to Philaenis," when Sapho, expounding the pleasures of Lesbian dalliance, finds a parallel in the movement of birds and fish. Men leave behind them, she says, that which shows their sin,

> But of our dallyance no more signes there are,
> Then fishes leave in streams, or Birds in
> aire.[17]

The same figure—but carried even further—appears in a verse letter to his friend, Sir Henry Wotton; make your life so self-contained, says Donne, and plan your way so carefully that you will pass along it as

> Fishes glide, leaving no print where they passe,
> Nor making sound.[18]

In such imagery, of course, actual observation is only an essence to which the writer makes a speculative addition before he uses it as analogy. The movements of fish may be the source of these figures but the conjecture concerning the effect of these movements is an imaginative contribution in itself; thus the poet plays imaginatively with his source even before he uses it.

We turn now to that company of images which draws upon the creatures and conceptions of folklore and hearsay; these, we find, range from slight exaggerations of actuality to the most absurd and fantastic superstitions. In the first class fall most of those figures which utilize the characteristics of chameleons, salamanders, scarabs, and scorpions, and even of such comparatively familiar creatures as swans, bear cubs, eagles, and moles. In the class of completely grotesque invention fall those dealing with phoenix, cockatrice, basilisk, unicorn, and, as it happens, elephant and mouse.

Bears, the theory was, gave birth to mere lumps—and thus Donne is once again supplied with an analogy for love: It is, he says in Elegie XVIII, a "bear-whelp born," which, if overlicked, becomes a monster.[19] Elsewhere he describes men of France in their dress as "changeable Camelions"; [20] and the salamander, popularly supposed to be capable of living indefinitely in fire, proves to be a fitting emblem, on the one hand, of the spiritual life of the sinner,[21] and on the other, of the physical life of sailors at the equator.[22] Having addressed the Earl of Somerset and his bride as "Blest payre of Swans," Donne, remembering the old tale of the dying swan, hastens to add, "may you . . . never sing";[23] and an even quainter notion concerning eagles prompts his fancy when he says of himself in a letter to Sir Henry Goodere that even if he committed no positive sin but simply sat still and meditated he would still be sinning—just as the eagle would be

> very unnaturall if because she is able to do it, she should pearch a whole day upon a tree, staring in contemplation of the majestie and glory of the Sun, and let her young Eglets starve in the nest.[24]

To express his sense of men's equality in death, of the grave that receives all without distinction—an idea that fascinated and made eloquent every preacher and almost every poet of the age—Donne in his *Essays in Divinity* juxtaposes the noblest of creatures with the lowliest, the most beautiful with the most revolting. If a prince be a lion, he cries out,

> and live by prey, and waste among cedars and pines, and I a mole and scratch out my bed in the ground, happy in this that I cannot see him; if he be a butterfly the son of a silkworm, and I a scarab the seed of dirt; if he go to execution in a chariot, and I in a cart or by foot, where is the glorious advantage?[25]

I quote this figure again in order that I may point out once more that the color, fervor, and imagination of such imagery indicates that the line between prose and poetry is sometimes entirely arbitrary.

We find ourselves deep in the realm of the unreservedly fantastic with the description of a father who, suspecting his daughter of entertaining a suitor he hates, enters the house

with glazed eyes,
As though he came to kill a Cockatrice.[26]

The common superstition concerning the cockatrice was that his eye was—to use Shakespeare's epithet—"death-darting," but Donne seems to be utilizing the less common idea that if anticipated the creature could be given its own medicine. A tale equally old and equally grotesque—that of mice creeping up the trunks of unwary elephants and eating their way to the brain—is revived in Meditation 12 to suggest how insidiously the vapor sickness kills its victims.[27] In "The Progresse of the Soule" Donne, outdoing himself in the direction of extravagant fancy, describes such an invasion in full detail.

Even primitive conceptions of generation play a part: thus, for example, the power of God's eye to bring great things out of us suggests the alleged ability of certain creatures to hatch their eggs by looking at them.[28] The creatures fabled to rise from the slime of the Nile become symbols of the nameless, the formless, the almost unspeakable: before repentance, Donne says, the sinner lies as we may suppose, "out of the authors of natural story,"

> the slime and mud of the river Nilus to lie, before the sun-beams strike upon it; which after, by the heat of those beams, produces several shapes, and forms of creatures.[29]

This is spontaneous generation clothed in the mysteries of old Nile. More familiar than this and perhaps most famous of legendary types of generation is that of the phoenix; Donne makes a nice distinction between it and other fabulous births when he declares that youth rising out of infancy or age out of youth is rather like wasp out of carrion or snake out of dung than phoenix out of the ashes of another phoenix.[30] But the birth of the phoenix was only one of the several unique and fantastic characteristic that made the bird a favorite in folklore and the source of more images in Donne than any other creature of popular fancy. Another strange habit attributed to the bird was that of building its own funeral pyre; thinking of this, Donne writes of a bride and groom that they are phoenixes in whom is kindled such fires

> as shall give
> Yong Phoenixes, and yet the old shall live.[31]

The equally fanciful notion that there is but one phoenix at a time turns up as a perfect representation of the man who thinks there is but one of his kind.[32] And finally, writing of that riddle of riddles, the love relationship, it is to the phoenix that he must turn for adequate parallel; he says to his beloved in "The Canonization":

> The Phoenix ridle hath more wit
> By us, we two being one, are it.
> So to one neutrall thing both sexes fit,
> Wee dye and rise the same, and prove
> Mysterious by this love.

None of these, it may be noted, gives adequate indication of how much of all this folklore Donne really accepted and how much he used only because it happened to be uniquely suited to his needs. On this score we have several images concerning credulity itself; although they are hardly decisive we cannot overlook them. In one, men who write of the Holy Ghost and the Trinity without knowing what these concepts mean are compared with those who write of phoenixes, unicorns, pygmies, and giants.[34] The inference seems to be that both are esoteric

bodies of knowledge and that both are only inadequately
understood. Even more provocative is the figure wherein
a father, smelling the good but exotic perfume of his
daughter's concealed lover, thinks it strange,

> as we in our Ile emprisoned,
> Where cattell onely, 'and diverse dogs are bred,
> The pretious Unicornes, strange monsters call,
> So thought he good, strange, that had none
> at all.[35]

Although this appears to be a criticism of any Englishman
who is unwilling to accept accounts of creatures he has
not seen, it seems to me to be intended more as a comment
on the general provincialism and bourgeois narrowness of
the average Englishman. Perhaps Donne prided himself on
his open-mindedness with reference to such exotic tales;
it is the kind of open-mindedness that sometimes makes
mental bedfellows of the receptive intellectual and the
gullible peasant. In any case it should be evident by now
that the fantastic aspects of such lore would hardly deter
him from using it, that its fancifulness was, in all prob-
ability, one of the elements which attracted him.

CONCLUSION

XXI

COMPARISONS AND INTERPRETATIONS

Although the very distribution and arrangement of the material in the preceding chapters is its own comment and although I have sought even in passing to make clear the significance of much of that material, we have still to see what all this means in the total picture of Donne the writer. We have still, too, to make adequate use, by way of comparisons, of the interesting image data on Shakespeare and other Elizabethans furnished by Professor Spurgeon's investigations.*

Although we cannot help being interested in the light which imagery can cast on biography, we must expect, of course, that the analysis of what Donne's imagery can tell us concerning the man himself will be far less profitable and satisfying than the study of what it contributes to his writing. Concerning the latter we can make thoroughgoing and definitive decisions; concerning the former we must remember that although imagery is a unique storehouse of subtle revelations of mind and personality it shares the natural limitations of creative writing in that such revelations are likely to be unsystematic and incomplete.

---

* In all such comparisons I have tried to make allowances for the differences in classification between Professor Spurgeon's system and mine. The most important of these are her treatment of "Domestic" and "Body" images as entities separate from "Daily Life," "Personifications" as separate from "Body" and part of a group of images called "Imaginative," sickness and its treatment as a part of "Body" images, and ships as a part of "Nature" imagery.

It should also be noted that such comparisons are based on proportionate relationships within each writer's imagery, since, for example, Professor Spurgeon's conclusions concerning Shakespeare are founded on about 7,300 images, mine concerning Donne on about 2,300.

The fact that looms up largest from a broad view of the whole body of Donne's images as I have arranged them is the importance of those in Part I—that is, of the figures issuing in one way or another from science or learning. Although the number of Donne's images from daily life is greater, it must be realized that the numerical preponderance of such images is to be expected in almost all writers, that it may be caused, as it is in Donne, by a host of casual or merely allusive figures, and that it is significant only when the preponderance is very great, as in Shakespeare or Bacon,* or when it is distinguished by imagery indicating really vital interest. In Shakespeare, as is made clear again and again,† images from nature and from daily and domestic life dominate completely, while those from learning and the sciences are comparatively unimportant. What this means is that where Shakespeare's imagination in quest of an analogy turns instinctively, as it were, to gardening or the weather, to a household custom or the expression on a human face, Donne's turns just as naturally to an astronomical concept, a proposition in geometry or a procedure from medicine. Where Shakespeare's imagery is constantly infusing into his work a vitalizing, infinitely human sense of the ways of men and the homely tasks of the daily round, and the most vivid glimpses of the natural world, Donne's brings in the intellectual flavor of science and miscellaneous professional learning. Where the former achieves the balance and completeness of a body in which heart, brain, stomach, muscles,

---

* See *Spurgeon,* Charts III and V. The indications are that the same decided preponderance holds true of the imagery of Dekker, Chapman, Jonson and Massinger. Marlowe's images appear to be an exception; they show, like Donne's, a very large proportion from learning, but differ sharply from Donne's in that they are taken for the most part from classical sources (see *Spurgeon,* Chart II) ; this gives an entirely different face to their effect.

† *Spurgeon,* pp. 13, 15, 44-45, 86, 112, 204, 205.

and nerves rule cooperatively, the latter suggests one wherein the brain dominates, transforming the contribution of each of the other organs into the image of its own.

In "Ideas of the Universe," the first of our divisions within Part I, we get evidence immediately, in varied and striking examples of Donne's imaginative interest in scientific ideas. In these images the theories and systems of the cosmologists are assimilated with understanding and completeness; subtle implications and abstruse distinctions are introduced and pursued until all the complex visions of the universe stand reflected in imagery. The images of both Shakespeare and Bacon, it is true, also show an interest in astronomy,* but not quite so great, I think, as Donne's. In theirs, moreover, the old Ptolemaic system dominates—a domination which Professor Spurgeon attributes in part to the fascination that the myth of Phaeton driving his horses across the sky had for the Elizabethan poetic mind. Myths had no such attraction for Donne, and, as we have seen, it was the new theory of the solar system and the radical changes which it brought with it that really stirred his imagination. Although the influence of Scholastic science on Donne's thought is sometimes made much of and although his imagery does touch familiarly on the *primum mobile,* the spheres, their intelligences, and the "unchangeable firmament," it is the revolutionary intellectual heresy of Copernicus and Galileo that evokes the most brilliant and elaborate of his metaphors. Marlowe's imagery, too, shows a very great interest in heavenly phenomena, but it is of an entirely different kind, revealing a preoccupation with the "dazzling heights and vast spaces of the universe"—symptomatic, as Professor Spurgeon describes it, of the man's "magnificent

---

* *Spurgeon,* p. 21.

surging upward thrust and aspiration" * rather than any absorption in astronomical theory or controversy. But more significant, I repeat, than the differences in the points of view between Donne and these others is the loving care and energy with which Donne worked out the images he drew from his conceptions of the universe; it is plain that such materials stimulated his fancy as did very few things in domestic life or the daily routine.

One of the most interesting facts concerning Shakespeare's images from medicine, Professor Spurgeon found, was that they clustered around everyday illnesses and their treatment, and thus associate themselves with imagery from daily life rather than with that from science or learning. In Donne, on the other hand, the predominance of figures from Galenist and Paracelsian medical theories, from anatomy and the techniques of surgery, from esoteric concepts like that of the body balm, and, finally, from alchemical science—or pseudo-science,— makes his medical images distinctly a phase of imagery from learning and science. Although Shakespeare's writing is of course not without many figurative elements from medical theory and Donne's not without many reflections of illness as it is connected with daily life, the difference in emphasis epitomizes the contrast between the imaginative directions of their imagery. Shakespeare is interested in illness because it is human; Donne is equally interested in medicine because it is, so far as imagery is concerned, a system of complex, exact, and rarely exploited theories. This, too, is among the reasons why Donne explores alchemy with such hydroptic curiosity; in so far as alchemy is "scientific," and to a certain extent bizarre, it is typical of the bypaths Donne's imagination constantly sought to explore.

---

* *Spurgeon*, p. 13.

Although it is shot through with a faint strain of the mystical, harking back to Aristotle and the Church Fathers, Donne's imagery from circles and geometric relationships suggests much the same observations. If anything, it illustrates even more clearly and completely his imaginative bent in the direction of the intellectual. What obviously attracts him among these things is the objectivity and exactness of the scientific fact—its capacity to clarify and crystallize the most nebulous spiritual concepts and the most amorphous emotions. And this is just what Donne makes these images do when he illustrates his notions of life, religion, and the Deity by means of circles, lines, and geometric configurations. It is here that Donne's imaginative originality and extraordinary mental agility make themselves felt most. Soaring into the rarefied upper regions of the fancy he brought down a group of parallels that are unique, peculiarly illuminating, and intellectually exciting in the way they perceive striking similarities in the otherwise dissimilar. Moreover, in his use of circles as produced by the mathematical compass he fuses his interest in the precision and objectivity of the scientific with an allied and almost equal interest in much the same qualities in things mechanical. This interest in the mechanical we shall have occasion to note again and again.*

Although we have seen evidence which indicates that Donne was, at least in his early years, interested in law, his images from this source seem at first glance to offer little support of this. There is a scattering of figures from remote-sounding legal procedures but although these represent that same tendency of Donne's toward the esoteric and the technical, it is demonstrable that many Eliza-

---

* It need hardly be noted that Professor Spurgeon's study reveals no similar interest in the circle or geometric forms in Shakespeare or in any other Elizabethan whose imagery she analyzed.

bethans used images from law and that legal jargon was in some literary quarters virtually a convention of love poetry. So conventional was such imagery and such jargon that Donne actually mocks a gull who uses them, and it is quite possible that although he had a semi-professional knowledge of law, and found its principles and processes interesting, he was unwilling to be guilty of a literary practice he had satirized. I feel that the sharply-drawn distinctions and clarifications which abound in legal theory and practice would have been peculiarly suited to his purpose; and this is substantiated by several of the legal images which actually appear in his work. Thus, although intimate with the material and surely aware that it filled his needs, his dislike of whatever smacked of the conventional or hackneyed seems to have been enough to make him avoid using that material to any significant extent.

From religion Donne drew, as I have pointed out, not as abundantly as one might expect. A partial explanation of this was seen in the fact that at the time of his early writings he had not yet developed any considerable interest in religion, while in his later years, when religious feeling became the inspiration of almost all his writing, he was not likely—so long as he accepted the principle that one of the most stimulating functions of imagery was to illuminate one idea by means of another not related to it in content—to illustrate such material with analogies from the same source. Although less important than expected, Donne's religious imagery tells us much that is interesting: most prominent of the things that it reveals is the fact that Donne applies it in most cases to the love of woman. Although profane love is one of Donne's major themes and some clustering of religious images around it might be expected, and although such a tendency is not unique among Elizabethan poets,* the extent to which he carries the association makes it one of the most conspicuous in his work. It results, in truth, in a veritable religion of love wherein the mistress is deity, sexual relations a holy mystery, and love poetry a ceremony of sanctification. When we find, in addition, that he occasionally illuminates religious themes with imagery from love and courtship, the entire relationship assumes the proportions of a fusion —or perhaps a confusion—between two worlds of feeling, the erotic and the religious, an interchange whereby Donne worships his mistresses with all the ritual of religious devotion and woos God with all the fervor of erotic passion. The final contrast is of the free-living cynical young writer of amatory verse revealing a definite imaginative interest in religious imagery and then of the reverend, intensely devout writer of divine poems showing a strong imaginative tendency to use the language of the sensual lover. The tendency of the young poet may be explained in some cases as a sincere attempt to spiritualize his open expression of sexual interest, in others as simply a cynical arrogation of sacred language and ideas to intensify profane avowals.

Classical mythology is, I think, as close to the heart of the tradition of Spenser, Sidney, Lyly, Lodge, and their followers in the next generation as any single phase of Elizabethan-Jacobean writing. It is difficult, in fact, to think of any creative source more insistently drawn upon by these writers for the purpose of metaphor or embellishment. Traditional by the time it had come to the Elizabethans and then rendered thoroughly hackneyed in the limitless outpourings of the sonneteers and song-

---

* It has, in fact, been connected with the Platonic but distinctly sensuous tradition of the religion of beauty in woman which flourished in Renaissance Italy. See Jefferson Butler Fletcher's *The Religion of Beauty in Woman,* N. Y., Macmillan, 1911.

writers, even the most famous of these fables and legends seems to have exerted virtually no attraction for Donne. His images from this source are as scanty, I dare say, as those in any writer of his time. The fact that there are but two score and that most of these are superficial references suggests their unimportance; it is made graphically clear when we learn that in Shakespeare * mythology is the source of about two hundred and fifty images (proportionately twice as many as in Donne), and that in Marlowe—coming closer to the Spenserian tradition—it produces by far the largest number of figures of any group in the poet's imagery † and augments his images from learning to such an extent that that category dominates for this reason alone. Donne's antipathy to the classical metaphor is not equivocal; not only is there a negligible number of detailed or vivid figures of this type but even the casual or fragmental figure—the kind that may well slip by hardly noticed by the writer himself—is not generously represented. If, as I have said, classical mythology is a hallmark of the Spenserian tradition, the nature of Donne's images from this source is the most convincing evidence of his revolt against that tradition.

It would be interesting to be able to deduce the exact nature of Donne's interest in the arts, but this, as it happens, is one of the places where the evidence supplied by his images is fragmentary and incomplete. In general they seem to suggest that he had an average, in no way exceptionally strong interest in, as well as knowledge of music, drama, and the visual arts; but the information yielded by them makes it hazardous to essay more positive or particularized conclusions. We observed that in his youth he frequented the theatre, but that as he grew

---

* *Spurgeon,* Chart V.

† *Spurgeon,* Chart I.

older and turned toward the church, and as the drama itself became decadent, this interest withered away. It was evident, too, that his appreciation of painting and sculpture, limited by the feeble or embryonic state of these arts in the England of his day, remained virtually undeveloped. Although the figures from music were more numerous, they revealed, characteristically enough, less interest in the beauties of musical sound than in the technicalities of the art and the physics of instrument construction. There appeared to be little of that sensitivity to harmony, discord, song, and the music peculiar to different instruments which is so abundant in Shakespeare.* The pleasures of music, the sensuous joy in sound which echoes and re-echoes through the lines of so many poets finds no voice in Donne. Frequently indifferent to conventional music and melody in his rhythms and metres, he is hardly less indifferent to these things in imagery.

Turning to the various divisions of Donne's imagery from daily life, we note again the fact of their greater number, but also, again, that this is to be expected in most writers and that in Donne it is due for the most part to many obvious and casual figures. In the writings of Shakespeare and Dekker, where it dominates overwhelmingly,† such imagery contributes the homely flavor and simple realism of daily life and the domestic routine, and all the humanity and warmth of men's faces and ways carefully observed and vividly reproduced. Casual as many of the images of this type may be in Donne, they might have contributed something of this same flavor were it not for a tendency in many of the most striking of them which shifts their emphasis and alters their general effect. That tendency is toward the mechanical and technical;

---

* *Spurgeon*, pp. 69–71, 74, 75, 76 and 270.
† *Spurgeon*, pp. 40–41 and 44.

and is, as I see it, closely allied to that which turns him toward imagery from learning and science. Like the latter, the mechanical and the technical can supply figures capable of crystallizing the spiritual or the emotional in superlatively clear and objective terms. They contribute to that air of precision of which even the casual reader of Donne becomes aware; and together these two tendencies form an essential phase of that intellectualism which is so important and peculiar a Donnean quality.

Looked at from another point of view, this preference for the technical or the mechanical might conceivably be interpreted as only one facet of a larger tendency—that wherein he turns to the least obvious source, or, if the source itself is familiar, to its least obvious aspects. When the material is commonplace he approaches it by some new path, pushes past the veil of familiarity which surrounds it, and usually manages to return with images from relationships or characteristics hitherto unnoted or unused. When the source itself is uncommon the images which he draws from it will obviously be intrinsically abstruse, remote-sounding or bizarre—as those, for example, which make use of electrum, bezoar, the structure of the cranium, or body balsamum. This whole tendency in Donne's imagery is striking and fairly pervasive, and is certainly considerable enough to render understandable Samuel Johnson's famous description—though perhaps not his estimate—of the "wit" of Donne and the "metaphysical" poets.

Of the proclivity toward the mechanical we have seen evidence among Donne's images from science and learning, as, for instance, in the groups of figures drawn from the geometer's compass and the distillation processes of the alchemist; but we note it even more conspicuously in "Domestic Life," the first of our chapters dealing with images from daily existence. Here, in a welter of fairly conventional figures taken from the routine activities * of the domestic round, one of the few patterns that stands out is that of imagery from watches and clocks—not watches and clocks in any usual sense but in terms of their mechanical construction and the technicalities of their operation. For the rest, the images of this chapter—dealing with buildings, the household, food, and clothes—are characterized by great variety but by little that is detailed or unusual or possessed of imaginative vitality. Those from household articles, furnishings and customs rarely attain the colorful realism of Shakespeare's,† and although Donne in a few instances shows himself capable of reproducing in the most lifelike and vigorous manner the homeliest of indoor scenes, these are exceptions. Those from clothing reveal interest in their style, quality and condition, an interest that seems to reflect the attitudes that the writer probably had as young-man-about-town, and, later, as pensioner on the fringe of the royal court. Those from food, finally, are too few to tell us much beyond the fact of their limited importance. If anything, the paucity of these food images seems to indicate a feebleness of interest in the taste sense which, when considered in conjunction with what we have learned of Donne's lack of interest in musical sound, suggests another deep-lying difference between the sources to which he and Shakespeare turned. Where many of the latter's most vivid and telling figures originate in the direct experience of the senses, in Donne the number of images that issues directly from such experiences is negligible. As additional confirmation of this it may be pointed out that Donne's images from colors or vividly colored objects are insignificant, and, in

---

* See *Spurgeon*, p. 114.

† *Spurgeon*, pp. 112, 114-116.

so far as these are indicative of interest in the visual,* his reliance on sight is apparently no greater than that on hearing or taste. Either Donne's sense impressions are meagre and of indifferent strength or intellect has done its work so well that all sensory details have been absorbed, transformed or shunted aside. The latter explanation is undoubtedly the more illuminating.

If the little group of images from sports and games tells us anything, it is that Donne, by the time he had completed the major part of his writing, had lost most of his interest in such activities—presuming, of course, that he had ever had such an interest. For all the frequently noted "masculinity" of such poems as his satires, one gets no feeling from his imagery of Donne himself as a virile follower of outdoor sports and the strenuous pastimes. Even the considerable group of images from fowling and falconry loses a little of its significance when we learn of the number and variety of the uses made of these sports in the works of Shakespeare and Dekker.† It interested Donne; the other two it fascinated. But after all it should be remembered that it is less important to decide whether Donne was or was not personally a follower of outdoor life and sports than to realize that in not having such imagery he lacks one of the elements which makes for the freshness, vitality and robustiousness characteristic of the work of Shakespeare, and, to a lesser degree, of Dekker.

Although it was apparently quite natural for the ordinary Londoner of Elizabeth's time to know something of ships, it is clear from Donne's biography that his experience with them was more extensive and intimate than that of the average citizen. To this his imagery adds the in-

---

* See *Spurgeon,* pp. 58–69.

† *Spurgeon,* Chart IV and pp. 30-33.

formation that his interest kept pace with his experience: a stream of images tells us that his imagination was stirred by almost all the aspects and associations of sea travel, navigation and exploration. And it tells us that once again the most conspicuous single tendency is a virtually pervasive one toward the mechanical. In fact, his images from navigation and the box-compass and from maps are among the most striking illustrations of this curious but insistent impulse of Donne's imagination. In their elaborate use of the abstruse and the esoteric they would be hard to parallel in any of our older poetry; they represent the main contributions of Donne's imagery to the knottiness and difficulty which troubles those reading his poetry for the first time. These, as Coleridge said, are the iron pokers which Donne wreathes into true-love knots. Besides this one, there are two dominant strains in his imagery from seafaring, the first contained in that sharply-drawn series of figures associating ships and sea travel with danger and inexorable disaster, and that interesting group which introduces the ways and deeds of the great explorers. The first association is certainly a memento of unhappy personal experiences with the hazards and hardships of typical Elizabethan ship travel—an association by no means uncommon at the time, but in Donne unusual in the variety and intensity of the images which establish it. The other stream of images, those from exploration or travel far afield, assumes added significance when we learn that they were conspicuously absent from Shakespeare's work and surprisingly negligible in that of Marlowe, Bacon, Massinger, Dekker, and Jonson.* Perhaps Donne's imaginative interest in these things came as a result of his contacts with Sir Walter Raleigh and the

---

* *Spurgeon,* p. 45 and Chart IV.

Honourable Company of the Virginia Plantation, perhaps as a result of both this and the underlying affinity between his own insatiable curiosity, boldness, and individuality—essentially intellectual though they were—and the temerity, defiance of tradition, and hunger for the new and wonderful that distinguished the Magellans, Drakes, Cavendishes, and Raleighs.

Although it is commonly felt—perhaps more so today than in Elizabethan times—that commerce and money represent the prosaic in life and are a barren realm as far as the poet's imagination is concerned, we find Donne, almost perversely it would seem, drawing on them repeatedly and, in some instances, with a certain amount of vigor. He did so probably because they were precise, usually sharply defined, and not yet rendered stale by over-use; but whatever be their attractions they add to that which is unconventional in his approach and serve to set him even further apart from the Sidneys, Lylys and Watsons of his time. It does not quite set him apart from Shakespeare, however, for the great playwright seems no more averse than Donne to using commerce, money, and the work of artisans when these offer parallels more illuminating than any from sources traditionally thought more poetic.* Furthermore, here again Donne's penchant for the technical plays its part. We find not only metaphoric excursions into the practices of jewellers, engravers, statuaries, and a dozen other artificers, but also an astonishing series of imaginative flights into all the theories and processes of coinage. In fact, it soon becomes evident that there is little so sacred to God or man that it cannot be illustrated by some phase of coinage, nothing so peculiar

---

*Nor does it set Donne entirely apart from Jonson and his building trades imagery (apparently inherited from his father), or from Dekker and his host of figures from shoemaking.

to the spirit that it cannot be illuminated by some aspect of minting, stamping, clipping, debasing or counterfeiting. Fascinated by coins—although perhaps least of all by the wealth and power which they epitomize for most men— Donne found in their origin, manufacture, use and abuse a world of symbolic meanings.

Throughout his youth and middle years Donne's relation to the court, as we have noted more than once, was that of the needy suitor for preferment. It was an ignominious quest, and, as it turned out, a not too successful one; in the course of it he had ample opportunity not only to look behind the scenes and see what went on behind the tinsel and glamour of the court but also to know intimately the wantonness of its disregard. It is hardly surprising, then, that out of such a biographical background should come images which turn again and again to the less savory aspects of kingship, court, and things of state. I should be inclined, perhaps, to suspect such a conclusion as tending to find the autobiographical in what may be partly or wholly literary, did I not feel that a writer is quite likely to reveal his truest feelings in his imagery—just because in that direction he does so most unwittingly. When a score of metaphors and similes, appearing over a period of as many years, turn to the unpleasant sides of court life and the ways of monarchs, they can hardly be construed simply as a convenient attitude or a literary pose. They seem to me a subtle revelation of disaffection—a disaffection that is perhaps occasionally implicit in his letters but of which we have of course no direct statement.

In approaching an age which accepted war unconditionally and practiced it apparently without qualms we must accustom ourselves to the idea that warfare and weapons will play a prominent role in the imagery of its poets.* In this direction there seems to be little that distinguishes Donne from his contemporaries; in fact, the most interesting of Donne's associations in this group, that between love and war, can apparently be paralleled in the work of many Elizabethans.† Moreover, although he never glorifies the martial spirit or indicates such open acceptance of the functions of war as does Bacon or even Milton, he is far from revealing anything of that feeling of abhorrence and contempt for war and its ways—so astonishingly in advance of his time and so vivid an index to his humanity—that marks the work of Shakespeare.** In this, once again, Shakespeare seems to stand absolutely alone. In Donne's images there is, in truth, little or no reflection of the writer's own feelings about these things; the human equation, the emotional reactions that war may arouse, are nowhere evident. Here as elsewhere Donne turns not to the human phase—men in battle or the ways of soldiers themselves—but to weapons and military procedures, that is, to the machinery or the mechanics of war.

In turning to images from metals and substances our expectation was that they would tell us something about the writer's sensory reactions—as similar groups of images tell us, for example, that Shakespeare was acutely conscious of the feel and texture of things, and that Marlowe reacted to their gleam, their brilliance, and general surface appearance.†† But no such information is forthcoming from Donne's images. What we have already concluded, on the one hand, of the unimportance of sense impressions in Donne's imagery, and, on the other, of his

---

* *Spurgeon,* pp. 36, 38–39.

† *Spurgeon,* pp. 38–39.

** *Spurgeon,* pp. 28-29 and 76.

†† *Spurgeon,* pp. 36-37.

tendency toward the technical, seems to be borne out conclusively when we find that in these figures from metals he shows little interest in their texture, hardly more in their appearance, but a great deal in their functions and properties. Here again it is the inobvious which attracts him; for the conspicuous strain among his images is that which issues from gold, not for any wealth or power it may suggest, or for any natural beauty, but because of its economic functions, its formation, ductility, tensile strength, and, most of all, its malleability—its capacity to be beaten into gold leaf. Thus, seeing gold in terms of its properties and functions, Donne once more transforms what might have been a revelation in sense reactions into a study—equally revelatory, to be sure—in the symbolism of the technical.

It is the lavish use of imagery and personification from the types and classes of mankind and from the human body itself that helps send through Shakespeare's pages a host of men and women as vital and varied as an Elizabethan throng,* and causes those pages to radiate a feeling of humanity, social sympathy, and living warmth unsurpassed in our literature. On the other hand, a writer like Marlowe shows little or no trace of such qualities; † in his imagery the feeling for human types, for men's faces and movements and characteristic ways, is at its faintest. These are the extremes; in between stands Donne—not unaware of such sources of imagery, capable of using them trenchantly and with no little verisimilitude, but actually doing so only infrequently. Although, as we have seen, a considerable variety of types is produced in these images of Donne's, there comes of them none of that sense

---

* *Spurgeon,* pp. 137–145.

† *Spurgeon,* pp. 35–36.

of closeness to living, breathing men and women which helps to make a literary work seem instinct with a human quality of its own. It is evident that although Donne observed men, and observed them keenly, he simply did not turn to them as did Shakespeare—as if they could supply an inexhaustible stream of quickening analogy. There is but one exception to this, an aspect of these figures from men and their characteristics that does contribute pungently to the flavor of Donne's work—and that is his imagery from death. It is out of this, as much as from any single source, that there issues that sense of man's mortality, decay everpresent, and the skull beneath the skin which pervades Donne's work and links him with that considerable group of Elizabethan and Jacobean writers whose works are shot through with the melancholy or morbid consciousness of death. The reasons why this sense of death should have been so extraordinarily pervasive in the early seventeenth century are complex; it is probable that many forces contributed: the tradition of the *carpe diem* theme; the fanatic emphasis of the medieval clergy on the vanity of the flesh; the depression and cynicism of spirit that seem to follow eras which, like the Elizabethan, are characterized by inordinate expansions in every direction; and life itself still rendered as cheap as ever by disease and war, the former raging unchecked, the latter accepted like daily bread. If some personal circumstance is needed to explain why Donne may have been even more sensitive to these forces than most men, we find it in his lifelong ill-health; it is the pathetic burden of his letters and the theme of his *Devotions;* in fact, Donne's images from this source are merely a sombre counterpoint in those lofty and impassioned fugues wherein he welcomes death, inveighs against the flesh, or dwells with almost pathological fervor on physical corruption and the ghastly work of the worm.

Although nature, as we have noted, was not an important theme in the poetry and prose of the sixteenth and seventeenth centuries—except perhaps for an occasional piece sounding with classical echoes,—its popularity as a source of metaphor and decorative effect was an old and well-established tradition. In the light of this, Donne's imagery from nature appears to be neither abundant nor memorable. Although studded here and there with passages which seize strikingly upon the bizarre or the uncommon, the images which represent his imaginative interest in flower, field, forest, and garden are for the most part conventional and faded; and although those from farm life show a somewhat more unusual emphasis on the sterner realities of that life, they, too, are not impressive. Any suspicion, moreover, that this avoidance of, or indifference to nature imagery was not unconscious seems to me at least partially confirmed by the several passages in which he makes clear his awareness of the fact that certain phases of this imagery had been sadly over-used. All in all these images offer few parallels to the varied and exquisitely wrought analogies which Shakespeare draws from the same source. It is not so much that Donne drew from the urban scene rather than from the rural or bucolic as that nature's most striking effects—just such as are recorded in Shakespeare's imagery—are for the most part simple and sensuous; and the simple and sensuous, as we have seen, does not get into Donne's writing unless he can discover or imagine something subtle or complex about it—whereupon it may appear, but so transformed that it is no longer simple and sensuous but recondite and intellectual. And nature imagery, finally, was bound up in certain directions with the pastoral tradition; as he avoided that tradition elsewhere, so here.

Similarly, the images Donne finds in the heavens, its luminaries, and in states of weather—as these are apprehended directly—seem to be of equally limited importance. They reveal but one aspect which arrests attention, and that is an acute consciousness of sunlight and shadow—a consciousness closely connected, it should be noted, with the very considerable interest in interior light and dark manifested in the images under "Domestic Life." The measured progress of shadow from morning to eve, the relation between shadow and that which casts it, the color of shade—these form another unique design in Donne's imagery. It is an interesting fact that these also exerted a peculiar fascination over Shakespeare's imagination,* but the difference is that Donne's images pursue the symbolism of shadows until they constitute an analysis almost scientific enough to warrant consideration among the images of Part I. Shakespeare was attracted by the pattern, the beauty, the play of light and shade, Donne by its causes, properties, exact relationships.

Donne's imaginative interest in the sea, if the images from this source may be considered together with those from sea travel, looms up larger than his interest in either of the phases of nature we have just examined. There is, to be sure, no sign here of any awareness of the sea's beauties, of the mysterious fascination it has been known to exert, or of any aspect involving really close scrutiny. His entire recall of it seems to be permeated by a sense of its dangers to man—obviously a reappearance of that strong association, noted earlier, between hardships and sea travel. Although such an association is plainly not unusual in an Elizabethan and although we find the same linkage in

---

* *Spurgeon*, Chart V and pp. 329–331, 310–315.

Shakespeare's imagery,* one feels that it is too vivid and insistent in Donne to be merely customary, and that, like the ship-travel images, it reflects his personal experiences and his own emotional reactions. Such comments do not, of course, apply to his images from rivers. These, too, are quite numerous and varied, and although few of them reveal the vigor and sharp observation that make so many of Shakespeare's river images memorable, they seem more nearly comparable to the great playwright's than those of any other Elizabethan studied by Professor Spurgeon.†

Last among our devisions are the images from animals and animal life. Somewhat overwhelming, of course, are the six hundred and thirty images from this source which can be found in the body of Shakespeare's work.** They represent, it is evident, an imaginative interest of the most extraordinary intensity and offer a chart of reactions that is as comprehensive and as clearly defined as any student of creative sources could hope for. Moreover, they establish beyond question the existence in Shakespeare of a sympathy for animals and a humaneness of attitude virtually unique among Elizabethan writers; †† in the manner of their reference to the limed or trapped bird, the hunted deer, the falcon mewed up, the bear at the stake, the over-spurred horse, and even the snail, they tell of a human spirit boundless in the quality of compassion. And by these tokens they indicate in a vivid way what is most lacking in the company—large as it is—of Donne's images from the same source. Once again we look in vain for some evidence of a writer's feelings and sympathies. In addition, draw-

---

* *Spurgeon*, p. 25.

† *Op. cit.*, pp. 94–96.

** *Spurgeon*, Chart V.

†† *Spurgeon*, pp. 27 and 32.

ing as most of them do from the more intimate and convincingly realistic aspects of animal life and behavior, Shakespeare's images set off in high relief Donne's tendency to use the most fantastic and grotesque of the creatures of popular fable. Although they, too, are not quite unique, these many figures from the animals of folklore, from phoenix and cockatrice, basilisk and unicorn, and from quaint notions of the more familiar creatures, form, in fact, one of the clearest examples of that imaginative inclination toward the bizarre and the strange. Although he never carried his unnatural natural history as far as Lyly and probably did not believe much of what he used, these queer conceptions of animals supplied him with a few analogies which are as outlandish as any in his work and could only have attracted him by their uniqueness.

Finally, once again we may point out how negligible are the differences between the imagery of Donne's prose and that of his poetry. If there is any difference it is solely one of manner: as we have repeatedly observed, the figures in prose tend toward diffuseness of statement, toward fullness, and even repetition. Where the minor term in Donne's verse images is generally condensed and elliptical—even when pursued through a succession of parallels—in the prose it is likely to be developed with a certain amount of rhetorical completeness. The image of poetry will seem to strike more suddenly, stimulating by its unexpectedness and exhilarating by its telescoping of thought and syncopated statement; by comparison the prose figure will occasionally seem pedestrian and lacking in spontaneity. That imagery plays a much more important part in Donne's poetry is evident from the fact that less than four hundred pages of verse yield as many figures as do more than three thousand pages of prose and that whole sermons move past virtually unlit by any flight of fancy while long poems explode with metaphors in every line. Nevertheless, in the final analysis Donne's imagery in the two media show no vital differences. When the metaphorical imagination does ignite in his prose it takes the same directions and reveals at bottom the same temperament as do the most effective images of his poetry.

These, then, are the observations which we may add, by way of supplement, to the conclusions implicit in the evidence of the preceding chapters. And in these, finally, we begin to see clearly the essential intentions of Donne's imagery. It is evident by now that in turning to learning and science, to the mechanical and the technical, and to the esoteric or the inobvious—for these, as we have seen again and again, are the larger tendencies of his imagery— Donne sought above all analogies which were precise, original, and uniquely illuminating. If they might at the same time surprise, that too was obviously desirable. Moreover, it is plain that he was often determined in his choice as much by what he wished to avoid as by what he actively sought; thus he turned away for the most part from figures that did not possess relatively clear outlines, that had lost impact from too much use, or had even begun to fade through over-exposure. This was why, in general, he eschewed the traditional sources of imagery, and why, moreover, he sometimes wandered far afield, wooing the bizarre and the strange.

Allowed the imaginative liberty of metaphor-making Donne sought to bring to bear on meaning parallels and similitudes which would lend the absolute clarity and precise definition characteristic of science, learned theory, and mechanical relationships. When this pursuit of figures intrinsically exact and perfectly parallel led him occasionally to the abstruse or the esoteric, he used them without hesitation, never dreaming, one suspects, that because of these very figures critics for centuries to come would charge him with being, of all things, wilfully obscure. What is not so obvious in Donne's turning to the scientific, the mechanical or the bizarre is the fact that he tended to avoid not only the cloudy and the hackneyed but all images with familiar emotional associations. In substituting for such images those which draw on circles, compasses, coinage, and clockwork—images, that is, notably free of emotional overtones of almost any sort—he produced perhaps the most essentially individual of his effects—the transmutation of feeling into objective symbols. It is not that Donne himself was in any way capable of less feeling than other writers, but that mind was so operative throughout the process of creation that the final statement of feeling is made in intellectual terms and primarily through images with a minimum of emotional implications. That such a transmutation of elusive emotional and spiritual attitudes into the scientifically defined and technically exact is a solution of uncertainties we are at leave to doubt. In fact, so persistent a tendency to seize upon the hard, bright, and mechanical in imagery may well suggest to some a personality flying from uncertainty—one which seeks escape from doubts by way of the superficially clear and the ostentatiously precise.

All this throws light on what has proved, fortunately or not, the most famous attempt to describe the Donnean image—Samuel Johnson's. We see in proper perspective that much-quoted passage in his life of Cowley in which—following paths of criticism suggested by Dryden, Pope, Hurd, Gray and others—he described the "metaphysical" conceit as *discordia concors;* a combination of dissimilar images, or discovery of occult resemblances in things ap-

parently unlike" whereby "the most heterogeneous ideas
are yoked by violence together." It must be remembered
that this was a summation intended to cover an entire
"race of writers," and that, as the specimens Johnson chose
indicate, Cowley and not Donne is the chief exemplar and
offender; at best it covers only one type of Donne's imagery, for the "metaphysical" conceit is, like the exposed
part of an iceberg, the most conspicuous but certainly not
the only kind of image in his work. Of the statement itself
the first thing that must be said is that it reveals a domination by canons of taste that make it difficult to accept
Johnson's estimate of any literary work in which imagination is an essential element. Although we may admire in
general the shrewdness and vigor with which he formulates
his convictions, and in this instance find a kernel of truth
in the phrase "discovery of occult resemblances in things
apparently unlike," Johnson is here a child of his time in
the sense that his point of departure in such criticism is
his adherence to propriety and his aversion to fancy and
individualism. It is a description of imagery phrased in
such a way that it might conceivably cover all metaphor
not using obvious and conventional parallels between ideas.
It declares, as does his repeated use of epithets like "far-
fetched," that Donne's analogies are brought from so great
a distance that they cannot be associated, except by violence, with the ideas they are supposed to clarify. But
such distance is relative: in part it depends on familiarity
—for an unfamiliar analogy will usually seem more "remote" than a traditional one,—and in part it is the difference between a critic whose canons did not permit his
imagination to accommodate easily and a writer who combined extraordinary interests with unique perceptivity.
Donne's nimble fancy given the liberty of the body of

knowledge which his prodigious intellectual appetite had furnished him and no such inhibitions as restrained neo-classicists, was bound to strike out many parallels which to Dr. Johnson could seem only queer, licentious or perverse. Johnson's prejudice is clear in the fact that several of the figures he uses to exemplify the work of these writers have always been accepted as among their most stilted and artificial; although he conceded that no one who wanted intellect or depended on an ability to imitate and copy could have been a "metaphysical" poet, he chose for the most part to exhibit them at their weakest and judge them by their worst. There is, moreover, no adequate recognition of the fact that in Donne, regardless of what may be true of Cowley and Cleveland, such imagery was the result not of whim and perversity but of an extremely analytical mind seeking to illuminate the most intense feeling.

Modern attempts to define the image retain the kernel of truth in Johnson's statements but make clear how narrow was his approach. At least two of these studies, those of Dr. Henry W. Wells * and Mr. George Williamson,† have analyzed carefully the technique of the Donnean image and in a general way its content. Dr. Wells bases his description on a definition of the figure as one wherein the two terms meet on a limited ground and are otherwise definitely incongruent, the minor term being significant only at a single, narrow point of contact. Checking this with what we have learned from the content of Donne's images we see it partly as an abstract statement of the tendency we described when we said of Donne that he sought always

---

* *Poetic Imagery,* Columbia University Press, 1924, chapter on "The Radical Image."

† *The Donne Tradition,* Harvard University Press, 1930. See especially pp. 32–34.

to use the least obvious aspect of the material to which he turned. By my wording I ventured to indicate explicitly what I thought was Donne's aim—to escape from the obvious and surprise with the unusual. To this definition, which is developed essentially from the point of view of the relationship between the terms, is added the equally significant ideas that the minor term is not usually poetic in the traditional sense and that, moreover, it tends away from the "romantic suggestiveness" which marks much conventional imagery. These, too, concur with our conclusions. They are fundamental distinctions and there is little to be added to them. We might, however, on the basis of our particular investigation push them further by pointing out that the minor term here is peculiar not simply in the fact that it is not conventionally poetic but that it definitely tends toward the learned, esoteric, and technical or mechanical, and that it does not simply avoid romantic suggestiveness but distinctly seeks to impersonalize as much as possible the emotional values in the major term. Further refinement of the description would, I think, begin to suggest that Donne's images were all cast in the same iron mould rather than that they show, like any embodiments of imagination, only general resemblances.

It may be pointed out, finally, that the information yielded by the content of Donne's imagery supports many latter-day interpretations of Donne's creative personality in general. It clarifies and supplements particularly such studies as have recognized Donne's literary iconoclasm and his rebellion against the Petrarchian tradition, his intense individuality, his ability to reproduce complex states of mind, and, above all, the constant unique interplay in his work between emotion and intellect, and the ultimate domi-

nance of mind.* It confirms—with such clearly defined
and objective evidence as they themselves do not often
possess—those recent analyses which recognize as the clue
to Donne's literary personality that profound and pervasive but subtle tendency to resolve emotional and psycho-
logical states into conceptual equivalents, that creative
alchemy whereby ideas are given passionate impact and
passion becomes objective. I refer especially to such interpretations because it is behind these that Donne's imagery
seems to throw its clearest and most conclusive evidence.

*   *

The final picture with which our study of Donne leaves
us is of a writer who forsook for the most part the accepted poetic beauties and the romantic overtones of
traditional imagery—particularly those of classical mythology and the world of nature; who forsook the charm of
both the simple and the sensuous, leaving the first for poets
like Herrick and the second for those like Keats, conscious that his own function lay elsewhere; who forsook,
though much less completely, the warmth and humanity of
the familiar and the common, finding more attractive that
which lay hidden beneath them; and who gave up, finally,
loveliness in general, because above all he worshipped
sense and intellectual meaning—those same gods to whom
he had sacrificed smooth metre and liquid rhythm.

For the effects which he had thus sacrificed he sub-
stituted others in their own way beautiful and among their
own kind unsurpassed. He replaced them with the pleasures of intellectual exercise, wherein difficulty provokes,
agility of wit and subtlety stimulate, and progressive solu-

---

* The most important of such earlier studies are those of Edmund
Gosse and Herbert J. C. Grierson; the most thorough of recent ones is
that of George Williamson; we may not overlook, however, the work done
in these directions by T. S. Eliot, Herbert Read, Mary Paton Ramsay,
Louis I. Bredvold, Mario Praz, Joan Bennett and Evelyn M. Spearing.

tion gives its own satisfaction; he introduced effects of surprise and shock that jolt into awareness and are tonic to the imagination; and for the cloudy traditional beauties he subtituted objectivity, clarity, and his own conclusions. His work is shot through as a result, with a freshness and originality in content as well as technique that has resisted with rare success the rust of time and imitation. And he achieved finally, by virtue of all these, an atmosphere of intellectual excitement and a pervasive imaginative electric almost unique in our literature.

APPENDIX

TABLE OF SOURCES

The following table of sources is intended to establish the breadth of the base upon which this study of Donne's imagery is founded. As I pointed out in the introductory chapter the number or mere quantity of images is of limited significance; the appended table must be approached in the light of the interpretation which has preceded.

The table is divided according to the titles and subtitles of the chapters of the text. It should be noted that of the total of 2,261 images 86 are duplicates resulting from cross-classification and 96 are vague or unclassifiable.

PART I

CHAPTER	NUMBER OF IMAGES	
III. IDEAS OF THE UNIVERSE		112
IV. MEDICINE AND ALCHEMY		
Medicine	116	
The Alchemical Quest	33	149
V. GEOMETRY AND THE CIRCLE		50
VI. LAW COURTS AND PRISONS		64
VII. RELIGION AND THE BIBLE		
Religion	99	
Bible Story	39	138
VIII. MYTH AND CLASSICAL STORY		57
IX. THE ARTS		87

PART II

PART III

KEY TO ABBREVIATION USED IN REFERENCES
TO DONNE'S WORKS

A—ALFORD, HENRY, editor, *The Works of John Donne,* London, John W. Parker, 1839 (6 vols.).

F—Facsimile of *Biathanatos,* New York, Facsimile Text Society, 1930.

G—GRIERSON, HERBERT J. C., editor, *The Poems of John Donne,* Oxford, 1912 (2 vols.).

H—HAYWARD, JOHN, editor, *John Donne's Complete Poetry and Selected Prose,* New York, The Nonesuch Press, 1932.

J—JESSOPP, AUGUSTUS, editor, *Essays in Divinity,* London, John Tupling, 1855.

K—KEYNES, GEOFFREY, editor, *Paradoxes and Problems with two Characters and an Essay of Valour,* London, The Nonesuch Press, 1923.

M—MERRILL, JR., C.E., editor, *Letters to Severall Persons of Honour,* New York, Sturgis and Walton, 1910.

Pseudo-martyr—*Pseudo-martyr,* London, Printed by W. Stansby for Walter Burre, 1610.

S—SPARROW, JOHN, editor, *Devotions on Emergent Occasions,* Cambridge University Press, 1923.

REFERENCES TO DONNE'S WORKS

NOTE: The matter in parentheses indicates the edition used and the page on which the passage appears. The volume number is added when the six-volume Alford text is referred to; it is not added for the two-volume Grierson text because only the first volume was actually used. The key to abbreviations used in referring to editions is given on the preceding page.

III. IDEAS OF THE UNIVERSE

1. (H. 361)
2. Letter (M. 37)
3. Ll. 7-10 (G. 336)
4. Letter (M. 23-24). See also the "Elegie upon Prince Henry," l. 90 (G. 270)
5. "The Extasie," ll. 50-52 (G. 53)
6. "A Feaver," ll. 21-24 (G. 21)
7. Respectively "Loves Growth," ll. 22-24 (G. 34) and Meditation 10 (S. 54)
8. Meditation 21 (S. 128)
9. Letter to Sir Henry Goodere (M. 88)
10. Ll. 205, 207, 209 (G. 237)
11. Letter (M. 53)
12. Verse Letter, ll. 37-40 (G. 196)
13. Sermon 18 (A. I, 347)
14. "Elegie upon Prince Henry," ll. 21-24 (G. 268)
15. Ll. 9-12 (G. 50)
16. *Biathanatos* (F. 146)
17. Epithalamion on the Lady Elizabeth and Count Palatine, ll. 39-40 (G. 128)
18. Verse Letter, "To the Countesse of Huntingdon," ll. 5-11 (G. 201)
19. "To Mr. Tilman," ll. 45-48 (G. 352)
20. Verse Letter, "To the Countesse of Bedford," ll. 67-68 (G. 197)
21. "A Funerall Elegie," ll. 67-70 (G. 247)
22. "The First Anniversary," ll. 117-120 (G. 235)
23. "Sapho to Philaenis," l. 60 (G. 126); "The Primrose," ll. 5-7 (G. 61); and Sermon 110 (A. IV, 517)
24. Sermon 75 (A. III, 354); and Sermon 24 (A. I, 494)
25. Paradoxe XII (K. 35)
26. "Loves Growth," ll. 15-18 (G. 33-34)
27. Ll. 204-205 (G. 139)

28. "The Progresse of the Soule," ll. 171-172 (G. 302)
29. Sermon 118 (A. V, 79) and Sermon 146 (A. V, 607). These are dated 1622 and 1627 respectively.
30. Sermon 2 (A. I, 25); Sermon 112 (A. IV, 568); and Meditation 1 (S. 2)
31. Sermon 112 (A. IV, 564 and Verse Letter, "To the Countesse of Bedford," ll. 41-42 (G. 196-197)
32. Respectively Sermon 81 (A. IV, 13); Sermon 9 (A. I, 179); Expostulation 3 (S. 13); letter to Sir H. Goodere (M. 40); and *Pseudo-martyr* (Ch. 4, p. 128)
33. Respectively Sermon 117 (A. V, 69); *Pseudo-martyr* (Ch. 4, p. 128); and letter to Sir Thomas Roe (H. 477)
34. Meditation 10 (S. 55)
35. Ll. 33-36 (G. 27)
36. Il. 9-10 (G. 65)
37. Verse Letter, "To the Countesse of Huntington," ll. 103-104 and 109-112 (G. 420-421)
38. "The First Anniversary," ll. 367-368 (G. 242)
39. Verse Letter, "To Sir Henry Wotton," ll. 29-32 (G. 181)
40. Verse Letter, "To the Countesse of Huntington," ll. 40-46 (G. 418-419)
41. Sermon 80 (A. III, 484)
42. "The First Anniversary," l. 206 (G. 237)
43. "The First Anniversary," ll. 235-236 (G. 238)
44. Holy Sonnet V, ll. 1-2 (G. 324)
45. Verse Letter, "To the Countesse of Huntington," ll. 97-98 (G. 420)
46. Meditation 8 (S. 42)
47. Ll. 1-2 (G. 279)
48. Ll. 13-14 (G. 168)
49. Meditation 1 (S. 2)
50. Meditation 4 (S. 16)

IV. MEDICINE AND ALCHEMY

1. Letter (M. 87)
2. (H. 396)
3. Verse Letter, ll. 59-62 (G. 182)
4. Elegie XX, ll. 15-16 (G. 122). See also Sermon 24 (A. I, 492-493)
5. *Biathanatos* (F. 216-217)
6. Letter to Sir T. Lucey (M. 12-13)
7. (H. 367)
8. Ll. 263-268 (G. 259)
9. Verse Letter, ll. 21-24 (G. 190)
10. "The First Anniversary," ll. 56-58 (G. 233)
11. Sermon 49 (A. II, 406)
12. Sermon 101 (A. IV, 343)

13. Letter to Sir H. G. (M. 84-85)
14. *Essays in Divinity* (J. 23)
15. "The Crosse," ll. 27-30 (G. 332). See also Sermon 11 (A. I, 217-218) and Verse Letter, "To Sir Edward Herbert at Julyers," ll. 40-42 (G. 195)
16. Sermon 98 (A. IV, 292)
17. "The First Anniversary," ll. 343-344 (G. 241)
18. Sermon 88 (A. IV, 122)
19. *Ignatius His Conclave* (H. 396)
20. Respectively Sermon 26 (A. I, 520) and Meditation 7 (S. 37)
21. (S. 37)
22. (J. 225)
23. *Pseudo-martyr,* Ch. 4, p. 129
24. Verse Letter, ll. 25-28 (G. 190)
25. "The Second Anniversary," ll. 127-130 (G. 255)
26. Respectively, "The Litany," l. 209 (G. 346); Verse Letter, "To the Countesse of Huntington," l. 32 (G. 418); and Elegie XX, "Loves Warre," ll. 13-14 (G. 122)
27. Ll. 53-55 (G. 177)
28. Ll. 209-211 (G. 346)
29. Respectively "Obsequies to the Lord Harrington," l. 126 (G. 275); Holy Sonnet III, l. 9 (G. 323) and Letter to Sir H. Goodere (M. 44)
30. (H. 396)
31. Sermon 60 (A. III, 54)
32. Sermon 54 (A. II, 508)
33. "The First Anniversary," ll. 435-438 (G. 244)
34. "A Valediction: of my name, in the window," ll. 23-24 (G. 26)
35. "The Second Anniversary," ll. 211-213 (G. 257)
36. "The Crosse," ll. 55-58 (G. 333)
37. *Essays in Divinity* (J. 23)
38. "Upon Mr. Thomas Coryats Crudities," ll. 53-55 (G. 173)
39. Ll. 40-42 (G. 35)
40. "Loves Growth," ll. 7-9, 11-12 (G. 33)
41. Ll. 12-15 (G. 44)
42. Verse Letter, "To Mr. Rowland Woodward," ll. 25-27 (G. 186)
43. *Essays in Divinity* (J. 122). See also Verse Letter, "To the Countesse of Bedford," ll. 16-20 (G. 199)
44. Respectively Verse Letter, "Henrico Wottoni in Hiberniae Belligeranti", ll. 13-15 (G. 189); "The First Anniversary," ll. 179-182 (G. 236); and "Elegie on the Lady Marckham," ll. 23 and 28 (G. 280)
45. Sermon 150 (A. VI, 67)
46. Letter (H. 439)
47. Sermon 62 (A. III, 100-101)
48. Sermon 28 (A. I, 563)
49. Sermon 154 (A. VI, 165)
50. "To E. of D. with six holy Sonnets," ll. 11-14 (G. 317)
51. Verse Letter, ll. 25-28 (G. 202)

52. Ll. 417-418 (G. 244)
53. Ll. 35-37 (G. 91). See also "The Progresse of the Soule," ll. 493-495 (G. 315)
54. Ll. 6-12 (G. 39). See also letter to Sir H. G. (M. 149)
55. Ll. 37-38 (G. 332)
56. Elegie XI, ll. 34-35 (G. 97)
57. Verse Letter, "To the Countesse of Bedford," ll. 28-30 (G. 219)
58. "The Undertaking," ll. 5-8 (G. 10)

V. GEOMETRY AND THE CIRCLE

1. (J. 234-235)
2. Sermon 79 (A. III, 443). See also Prayer 4 (S. 22) and note.
3. Ll. 23-24 (G. 61)
4. Sermon 2 (A. I, 27)
5. *Essays in Divinity* (J. 99-100)
6. Prayer 1 (S. 4)
7. "Upon the Translation of the Psalmes," ll. 1-4 (G. 348)
8. Sermon 2 (A. I, 28)
9. Sermon 61 (A. III, 76)
10. Ll. 435-439 (G. 264)
11. Sermon 135 (A. V, 426)
12. Verse Letter, "To the Countesse of Bedford," ll. 46-68 (G. 220)
13. *Essays in Divinity* (J. 99)
14. Sermon 25 (A. I, 502)
15. Sermon 12 (A. I, 239-240)
16. Letter to the R: Honorable Sir Thomas Roe (H. 476)
17. Sermon 79 (A. III, 468)
18. Expostulation 20 (S. 123-124)
19. Ll. 105-110 (G. 274)
20. Sermon 81 (A. IV, 4)
21. Sermon 25 (A. I, 502)
22. Sermon 154 (A. VI, 150)
23. Ll. 25-36 (G. 50-51)
24. "The Second Anniversary," ll. 507-508 (G. 266)
25. *Ibid.*, ll. 141-142 (G. 255)
26. Ll. 19-20 (G. 267)
27. Letter to Sir H. G. (M. 141)
28. "Obsequies to the Lord Harrington," ll. 67-68 (G. 273)
29. Letter to Sir H. G. (M. 54)
30. "The Second Anniversary," ll. 131-134 (G. 255)

VI. Law Courts and Prisons

1. Letter to G[eorge]. G[errard]., dated April 1612 (H. 463)
2. Ll. 45-57 (G. 151-152)
3. *Essays in Divinity* (J. 213)
4. "Ecclogue. 1613," ll. 87-88 (G. 134)
5. Ll. 10-13 (G. 34)
6. Ll. 22-24 (G. 55)
7. Ll. 37-40 (G. 31)
8. Satyre II, ll. 67-68 (G. 152)
9. *Ibid.*, ll. 72-73
10. Elegie IV, ll. 1-5 (G. 84)
11. Satyre II, ll. 11-14 (G. 150)
12. Elegie, "Death," l. 6 (G. 285)
13. Sermon 4 (A. I, 77) and "The Progresse of the Soule," ll. 66-67 (G. 297)
14. Verse Letter, ll. 59-60 (G. 197)
15. Sermon 4 (A. I, 77) and Sermon 158 (A. VI, 291)
16. Sermon 3 (A. I, 41)
17. Sermon 158 (A. VI, 291)
18. Letter to Sir H. G. (M. 28)
19. Meditation 3 (S. 10-11)
20. Expostulation 3 (S. 12-13)
21. Letter to Sir H. Goodere (M. 52)
22. Letter to Sir Robert Karre (M. 214)
23. Respectively Verse Letter, "The Storme," ll. 17-18 (G. 175) and Sermon 158 (A. VI, 282)
24. Sermon 25 (A. I, 500)
25. Sermon 149 (A. VI, 51)
26. "The Comparison," ll. 31-32 (G. 91)
27. Respectively "Loves Exchange," ll. 41-42 (G. 75) and *Essays in Divinity* (J. 172-173)
28. Holy Sonnet IV, ll. 5-8 (G. 323)
29. Letter to Sir H. G. (M. 139)
30. "Sapho to Philaenis," ll. 39-40 (G. 125)

VII. Religion and the Bible

1. "A Valediction: forbidding mourning," ll. 7-8 (G. 50)
2. "A Valediction: of the booke," ll. 15-16, 28-29 (G. 31)
3. Ll. 35-36 (G. 15)
4. Verse Letter, "To Mr. C. B.," l. 12 (G. 208)
5. Ll. 17-20 (G. 59)
6. Elegie XII, ll. 15-20 (G. 100-101)
7. Ll. 1-5 (G. 70)

8. Ll. 23-25 (G. 13)
9. Ll. 22-23 (G. 54)
10. Ll. 41-42, 44-46 (G. 89)
11. Respectively Elegie XIX, l. 18 (G. 120); and "Epithalamion made at Lincolnes Inne," ll. 74-75 (G. 143)
12. Elegie VIII, l. 50 (G. 92)
13. Ll. 88-89 (G. 144)·
14. Respectively Elegie III, ll. 1-4 (G. 82); Elegie VI, l. 13 (G. 88); and Elegie I, l. 26 (G. 80)
15. L. 10 (G. 331)
16. Ll. 12-14 (G. 330)
17. Ll. 25-28 (G. 353)
18. Ll. 9-14 (G. 328)
19. Ll. 9-10 (G. 328)
20. Verse Letter, ll. 69-70 (G. 203)
21. Verse Letter, ll. 4-8, 11-12 (G. 221)
22. Verse Letter, ll. 31-38, 43-44, 47-48 (G. 192)
23. Verse Letter, ll. 1-2, 16-18 (G. 189-190)
24. Verse Letter, ll. 14-15 (G. 218)
25. Verse Letter, ll. 61-64 (G. 193)
26. Verse Letter, "To the Countesse of Bedford," ll. 13-16 (G. 196)
27. Ll. 200-203 and 208-210 (G. 166)
28. (M. 231)
29. Verse Letter, "To Mr. R. W.," ll. 2-4 (G. 207)
30. "The Second Anniversary," ll. 169-172 (G. 256)
31. Meditation 3 (S. 10-11)
32. L. 27 (G. 146)
33. L. 10 (G. 150)
34. Verse Letter, ll. 39-45 (G. 225)
35. "The Litanie," ll. 28-31 (G. 339)
36. Elegie XV, ll. 39-40 (G. 109)
37. Verse Letter, "The Calme," ll. 34-35 (G. 179)
38. "The Second Anniversary," ll. 417-420, 423-424 (G. 263)
39. Verse Letter, "The Calme," ll. 27-28 (G. 178-179)
40. Elegie, "Death," ll. 45-47 (G. 286)
41. Verse Letter, "To Mr. R. W.," ll. 20-21 (G. 210). See also Letter (H. 439)
42. *Essays in Divinity* (J. 190-191)
43. Verse Letter, ll. 13-14 (G. 201)

VIII. MYTH AND CLASSICAL STORY

1. Ll. 15, 19-20, 23-26, 29-30 (G. 105)
2. Ll. 17-18 (G. 101)
3. Elegie VIII, ll. 21-22 (G. 91)

4. Ll. 7-8 (G. 100)
5. Elegie XVII, ll. 59-61 (G. 115)
6. Verse Letter, "To Mr. I. L.," l. 6 (G. 212)
7. "The Second Anniversary," ll. 27-29 (G. 252)
8. Elegie XX, ll. 17-18 (G. 122)
9. Meditation 4 (S. 17)
10. Ll. 23-24 (G. 91)
11. Ll. 35-38 (G. 121)
12. Ll. 129-130 (G. 163)
13. Verse Letter, "To Mr. S. B.," ll. 9-10 (G. 211)
14. Elegie XVIII, ll. 55-56 (G. 118)
15. Ll. 7-8 (G. 78)
16. Epithalamion on the Lady Elizabeth and Count Palatine, ll. 67-68 (G. 129)
17. Elegie IV, ll. 27-28 (G. 85)
18. L. 71 (G. 174)
19. "A Valediction: of the booke," ll. 5-9 (G. 30)
20. Ll. 31, 33-34 (G. 85)
21. "The Progresse of the Soule," l. 153 (G. 301)
22. Elegie IX, ll. 29-30 (G. 93)
23. Ll. 215-216 (G. 140)
24. *Essays in Divinity* (J. 111-112)

IX. THE ARTS

1. Verse Letter, l. 41 (G. 184)
2. "A Funerall Elegie," ll. 27-29 (G. 246)
3. "Upon the Translation of the Psalmes," ll. 15-16 (G. 348)
4. Sermon 40 (A. II, 221)
5. Sermon 9 (A. I, 176-7)
6. Ll. 1-5 (G. 368)
7. Satyre I, ll. 77-78 (G. 148)
8. (H. 442)
9. Letter to Sir Thomas Roe (M. 36-37)
10. "The Second Anniversary," ll. 90-92 (G. 253-254)
11. *Ibid.,* ll. 19-20 (G. 251)
12. Verse Letter, "The Storme," ll. 55-56 (G. 177)
13. Letter to Sir H. G. (M. 61)
14. Letter to Mrs. Martha Garet (M. 35)
15. "To Mr. E. G.," ll. 7-8 (G. 209)
16. Ll. 11-16 (G. 150)
17. Sermon 36 (A. II, 143)
18. Sermon 112 (A. IV, 570-571)
19. Respectively Verse Letter, "The Calme," l. 33 (G. 179) and Letter (H. 461)

20. Verse Letter, ll. 23-24 (G. 181)
21. Elegie XVI, ll. 35-36 (G. 112)
22. Verse Letter, "The Calme," l. 14 (G. 178)
23. Letter (H. 439)
24. *Ibid.*
25. Verse Letter, ll. 93-94 (G. 420)
26. Verse Letter, "The Storme," ll. 3-5 (G. 175)
27. Elegie XV, ll. 57-58 (G. 110)
28. Sermon 71 (A. III, 269)
29. Sermon 31 (A. II, 22)
30. Respectively Sermon 59 (A. III, 36); Sermon 62 (A. III, 84), and Sermon 148 (A. VI, 19)
31. Meditation 17 (S. 97)

X. Domestic Life

1. Holy Sonnet, "Nativitie," l. 5 (G. 319)
2. "The Progresse of the Soule," l. 181 (G. 302)
3. Meditation 18 (S. 104-105)
4. "The Progresse of the Soule," l. 393 (G. 311)
5. Sermon 37 (A. II, 160)
6. Sermon 124 (A. V, 207)
7. Sermon 26 (A. I, 533)
8. Sermon 12 (A. I, 236-237)
9. Sermon 95 (A. IV, 238)
10. "The Second Anniversary," l. 296 (G. 259)
11. Sermon 49 (A. II, 411)
12. Sermon 150 (A. VI, 61)
13. "A Valediction: of my name, in the window," ll. 28-30 (G. 26)
14. Sermon 80 (A. III, 482)
15. Letter to Sir H. G. (M. 55)
16. Sermon 100 (A. IV, 319)
17. "The Litanie," ll. 24-26 (G. 339)
18. "The First Anniversary," l. 448 (G. 244) and Elegie X, l. 24 (G. 95)
19. "A Funerall Elegie," ll. 73-74 (G. 247)
20. "The Second Anniversary," ll. 216-218 (G. 257)
21. *Ibid.,* ll. 85-88 (G. 253)
22. "The Canonization," l. 21 (G. 15)
23. "The Dreame," ll. 27-29 (G. 38)
24. "Ecclogue. 1613," ll. 29-32 (G. 132)
25. Letter (H. 442)
26. Meditation 23 (S. 139)
27. Expostulation 22 (S. 136)
28. Expostulation 1 (S. 3-4)
29. "A Funerall Elegie," ll. 37-40 (G. 246)

30. Sermon 53 (A. II, 492)
31. Sermon 122 (A. V, 175)
32. Ll. 131-146, 149-154 (G. 276)
33. *Essays in Divinity* (J. 48-49)
34. Verse Letter, "The Calme," ll. 8-9 (G. 178)
35. Verse Letter, ll. 55-57 (G. 223)
36. Sermon 13 (A. I, 267)
37. Sermon 141 (A. V, 525)
38. Sermon 52 (A. II, 461)
39. Sermon 80 (A. III, 469)
40. "The Second Anniversary," ll. 93-95 (G. 254)
41. Satyre II, ll. 81-84 (G. 153)
42. Satyre I, ll. 59-64 and 54-55 (G. 147)
43. Elegie II, l. 56 (G. 82)
44. Ll. 111-112 (G. 154)
45. Elegie II, ll. 33-34 (G. 81)
46. L. 28 (G. 337)
47. Letter to Sir H. G. (M. 53)
48. Ll. 355-356 (G. 242)
49. "The Extasie," ll. 7-8 (G. 51)
50. Ll. 208-210 (G. 257)
51. Sermon 70 (A. III, 255)
52. (K. 5)
53. (M. 55)
54. Sermon 136 (A. V, 446)
55. Satyre V, ll. 41-42 (G. 169)
56. "Newes from the very Countrey" (H. 413)

XI. SPORTS AND GAMES

1. "Loves Diet," ll. 25-30 (G. 56)
2. "Elegie on Mistris Boulstred," ll. 31-34 (G. 283)
3. *Essays in Divinity* (J. 189)
4. "News from the very Countrey" (H. 414)
5. Sermon 44 (A. II, 308)
6. Sermon 95 (A. IV, 230)
7. Sermon 2 (A. I, 24)
8. Satyre IIII, ll. 195-196 (G. 166)
9. Sermon 2 (A. I, 24) and Satyre II, ll. 45-46 (H. 125)
10. "News from the very Countrey" (H. 414)
11. Verse Letter, "The Calme," ll. 43-46 (G. 179)
12. Satyre IIII, ll. 233-234 (G. 167)
13. Paradoxe I, (K. 3)
14. Letter (H. 442)
15. Letter (H. 465)

16. Verse Letter, "To Sir Henry Wotton," ll. 23-24 (G. 188)
17. "The Progresse of the Soule," ll. 114-117 (G. 299). See also Sermon 4 (A. I, 73) and Verse Letter, "To the Countesse of Huntingdon," ll. 113-114 (G. 421)

XII. SEA TRAVEL AND EXPLORATION

1. Satyre III, ll. 17-19 (G. 155)
2. Elegie XX, ll. 21-22, 25-26 (G. 122-123)
3. (M. 68)
4. Letter (H. 472)
5. Prayer 23 (S. 147)
6. Ll. 7-9 (G. 180)
7. Letter to Sir H. Goodere (M. 44)
8. *Biathanatos* (F. 110-111)
9. Sermon 153 (A. VI, 120)
10. Sermon 120 (A. V, 127)
11. *Essays in Divinity* (J. 28-29)
12. Sermon 89 (A. IV, 141)
13. *Essays in Divinity* (J. 176-177)
14. Sermon 74 (A. III, 340)
15. Verse Letter, "To the Countesse of Huntingdon," l. 118 (G. 421)
16. Verse Letter, "The Storme," ll. 57-58 (G. 177)
17. "Aire and Angels," ll. 15-18 (G. 22). See also "The Second Anniversary," ll. 316-317 (G. 260)
18. "The First Anniversary," ll. 286-288 (G. 240)
19. "The Second Anniversary," ll. 7-8 (G. 251)
20. Sermon 4 (A. I, 65-66)
21. *Essays in Divinity* (J. 48-49). See also *Pseudo-Martyr,* Ch. 4, p. 121 for a strikingly similar image.
22. "The Annuntiation and Passion," ll. 25-28 (G. 335)
23. Sermon 67 (A. III, 186)
24. Ll. 223-226 (G. 238)
25. Sermon 125 (A. V, 251)
26. "A Valediction: of the booke," ll. 59-63 (G. 32)
27. "Obsequies to the Lord Harrington," ll. 111-118 (G. 274-275)
28. (H. 392)
29. Ll. 25-27 (G. 120)
30. "The Good-Morrow," ll. 12-14 (G. 7)
31. *Essays in Divinity* (J. 49)
32. Verse Letter, "To Sir Henry Wotton," ll. 13-15 (G. 187)
33. Ll. 68-70 (G. 197-198)
34. Sermon 22 (A. I, 445-6)
35. Verse Letter, ll. 53-54 (G. 419)
36. Letter (H. 467)
37. Ll. 41-72 (G. 117-118)

38. Ll. 7-15 (G. 368)
39. Sermon 25 (A. I, 502)
40. "The Annuntiation and Passion," ll. 19-22 (G. 334)
41. Sermon 53 (A. II, 499)
42. Sermon 66 (A. III, 175)

XIII. Commerce and Coinage

1. Letter (H. 467)
2. "The Annuntiation and Passion," ll. 45-46 (G. 336)
3. Holy Sonnet XVI, ll. 1-4 (G. 329)
4. L. 19 (G. 109)
5. "Lovers Infinitenesse," ll. 7-8, 16-17 (G. 17)
6. Ll. 93-94 (G. 130)
7. Letter to Mrs. Cokayn (H. 500)
8. Meditation 18 (S. 102-103)
9. Verse Letter, ll. 31-33 (G. 186)
10. Meditation 8 (S. 42). See also Letter to Sir H. G. (M. 74) and Sermon 88 (A. IV, 131-132)
11. Sermon 96 (A. IV, 250). See also Verse Letter, "To Lady Bedford," ll. 33-34 (G. 228); "The First Anniversary," ll. 229-232 (G. 238); "The Second Anniversary," ll. 228-230 (G. 258)
12. Verse Letter, "To Mr. E. G.," ll. 16-18 (G. 209)
13. "To Mr. Tilman," ll. 9-12 (G. 351)
14. Satyre IIII, ll. 188-190 (G. 165)
15. Holy Sonnet XV, ll. 9-10 (G. 329)
16. (J. 225)
17. Sermon 71 (A. III, 269)
18. Sermon 29 (A. I, 580)
19. "The Crosse," ll. 33-36 (G. 332)
20. "A Valediction: of weeping," ll. 1-4 (G. 38)
21. Elegie X, ll. 2-5 (G. 95)
22. Ll. 369-370 (G. 262)
23. Sermon 53 (A. II, 480)
24. (J. 200)
25. Ll. 13-18 (G. 351)
26. Ll. 429-431 (G. 263)
27. Sermon 85 (A. IV, 74)
28. Sermon 151 (A. VI, 85)
29. Respectively Sermon 108 (A. IV, 475) and Sermon 83 (A. IV, 40)
30. Meditation 13 (S. 75)
31. Letter to Sir H. G. (M. 85)
32. Sermon 36 (A. II, 143)
33. Sermon 56 (A. II, 563)
34. Letter (H. 439-440)

XIV. KING, STATE, AND WAR

1. Meditation 12 (S. 69-70)
2. Meditation 10 (S. 55-56)
3. Ll. 25-26 (G. 25)
4. Ll. 27-32 (G. 80)
5. Ll. 69-70 (G. 152)
6. Meditation 11 (S. 61)
7. (H. 390)
8. Elegie IV, ll. 43-44 (G. 85)
9. Elegie XI, ll. 23-24 (G. 97)
10. Holy Sonnet IV, ll. 3-4 (G. 323)
11. Elegie, "Death," ll. 9-10 (G. 285)
12. Elegie XIV, ll. 29-30 (G. 106)
13. "Loves Growth," ll. 25-28 (G. 34)
14. "The Progresse of the Soule," ll. 136-139 (G. 300)
15. Ll. 360-375 (G. 261-262)
16. Ll. 1, 3-5, 29-34, 37-38, 43-46 (G. 122 and 123)
17. L. 15 (G. 49)
18. Ll. 13-14 (G. 51)
19. Ll. 24-28 (G. 35)
20. Holy Sonnet XIV, ll. 5-8 (G. 328)
21. (S. 55-56)
22. Meditation 11 (S. 60-61)
23. Respectively Meditation 19 (S. 111) and Meditation 1 (S. 1)
24. Meditation 19 (S. 112)
25. Verse Letter, ll. 10-15 (G. 187)
26. (J. 160-161)
27. Respectively the "Preface," par. 26; and Ch. 4, pp. 127-128
28. Respectively Ch. 10, p. 264; and "The Epistle Dedicatorie," A2-A3
29. Ll. 181-183 (G. 256)
30. Ll. 22-24 (G. 65)
31. Respectively "The Progresse of the Soule," ll. 312-313 (G. 307); and Verse Letter, ll. 16-18 (G. 218)
32. Ll. 3-4 (G. 44)
33. Ll. 1-2, 7-8 (G. 48)
34. Respectively "The Litany," l. 128 (G. 343); and "Newes from the very Countrey" (H. 414)
35. Respectively Expostulation 16 (S. 94) and Sermon 10 (A. I, 205-206)

XV. METALS AND SUBSTANCES

1. Elegie XVIII, ll. 9-16 (G. 116)
2. Verse Letter, "To the Lady Bedford," ll. 35-38 (G. 228)
3. Sermon 75 (A. III, 350)

4. Sermon 40 (A. II, 221)
5. Sermon 69 (A. III, 234)
6. Sermon 85 (A. IV, 74)
7. Sermon 108 (A. IV, 478)
8. *Biathanatos* (F. 155)
9. Ll. 21-24 (G. 50)
10. Verse Letter, "To the Lady Bedford," ll. 36-40 (G. 228)
11. Sermon 14 (A. I, 282)
12. Verse Letter, "To the Countesse of Huntington," ll. 25-26 (G. 202); and Verse Letter, "To Lady Carey and Mrs. Essex Riche," ll. 31-32 (G. 222)
13. Verse Letter, "To the Countesse of Salisbury," ll. 17-18 (G. 224)
14. "The Second Anniversary," ll. 241-243 (G. 258)
15. Sermon 149 (A. VI, 41-42)
16. Sermon 68 (A. III, 205)
17. Sermon 88 (A. IV, 122)
18. Ll. 13-14 (G. 291)
19. "Elegie on the Lady Marckham," ll. 20-22 (G. 280)

XVI. MEN AND CHARACTERISTICS

1. Ll. 203-204 (G. 237)
2. Verse Letter, "To Mrs. M. H.," ll. 21-22 (G. 217)
3. "Farewell to Love," ll. 12-15 (G. 70)
4. Ll. 75-76 (G. 148)
5. "A Funerall Elegie," ll. 51-52 (G. 247)
6. Ll. 53-56 and 59-64 (G. 147)
7. Ll. 38-39 (G. 156)
8. Ll. 62-64 (G. 152)
9. Verse Letter, ll. 4-9 (G. 206)
10. (H. 413)
11. Sermon 129 (A. V, 311)
12. Ll. 43-68 (G. 156-157)
13. Ll. 2-4 (G. 330)
14. "The Second Anniversary," ll. 85-88 (G. 253)
15. Letter to Sir H. G. (M. 28)
16. Sermon 146 (A. V, 605)
17. Verse Letter, "To Mr. B. B.," ll. 13-14 (G. 213)
18. Letter [To Sir Henry Wotton?] (H. 440)
19. Satyre II, ll. 21-22 (G. 150)
20. Satyre IIII, l. 164 (G. 164)
21. "The Sunne Rising," ll. 1 and 5 (G. 11)
22. Satyre V, ll. 74-78 (G. 170-171)
23. Sermon 137 (A. V, 466)
24. (S. 35)

25. (H. 501)
26. (M. 44)
27. Meditation 4 (S. 16)
28. Ll. 22-26 and 15-19 (G. 88)
29. Sermon 112 (A. IV, 564)
30. "The Extasie," ll. 2-3 (G. 51)
31. Elegie IV, ll. 51-52 and 41-42 (G. 85)
32. L. 99 (G. 234)
33. L. 42 (G. 109)
34. Ecclogue, l. 3 (G. 131)
35. Elegie XI, l. 56 (G. 98)
36. Verse Letter, "To Mr. T. W.," ll. 1-4 (G. 205)
37. Probleme II (K. 42)
38. Ll. 1-6 (G. 55)
39. Ll. 17-19 (G. 168)
40. Ll. 22-25 (G. 246)
41. (S. 69)
42. Ll. 7-8 (G. 145)
43. Sermon 158 (A. VI, 282)
44. Ll. 1-5 (G. 49-50)
45. Sermon 80 (A. III, 489)
46. Verse Letter, "To Sir H. W. at his going Ambassador to Venice," ll. 15-16 (G. 215)
47. Epithalamion on the Lady Elizabeth and Count Palatine, ll. 77-78 (G. 130)
48. "The Paradox," ll. 5-6 (G. 69). See also ll. 9-14 here.
49. "Epithalamion made at Lincolnes Inne," ll. 79-80 (G. 143)
50. *Ibid.*, 85-88 (G. 144)
51. "A Nocturnall Upon S. Lucies Day," ll. 21-22 (G. 44)
52. *Ibid.*, ll. 26-27
53. "Loves Alchymie," l. 24 (G. 40)
54. "The Second Anniversary," ll. 19-20 (G. 251)
55. *Ibid.*, ll. 13-17 (G. 251)
56. Sermon 108 (A. IV, 482)
57. Verse Letter, "The Storme," ll. 45-49 (G. 176)
58. "The Will," ll. 50-51 (G. 58)
59. Verse Letter, "To Mr. E. G.," ll. 9-10 (G. 209)
60. L. 115 (G. 163)
61. Meditation 19 (S. 111)
62. See Sermon 59 (A. III, 34-35; Sermon 158 (A. VI, 283) ; and Sermon 56 (A. II, 552)

XVII. NATURE

1. Ll. 3-7 (G. 224)
2. "Sapho to Philaenis," ll. 21-24 (G. 124-125)

3. Letter to G. G. (M. 207)
4. Sermon 9 (A. I, 176-177)
5. Sermon 112 (A. IV, 564)
6. Verse Letter, "To the Countesse of Bedford," ll. 15-18 (G. 191)
7. Sermon 73 (A. III, 326)
8. Song, l. 2 (G. 8)
9. Elegie upon Prince Henry, ll. 53-54 (G. 269)
10. "Twicknam Garden," l. 7 (H. 20)
11. Ll. 27-29 (G. 91)
12. "The Apparition," ll. 11-12 (G. 48)
13. Letter to Sir H. G. (M. 99)
14. "Elegie on the L. C.," ll. 9-13 (G. 287)
15. (S. 111-112)
16. Meditation 22 (S. 133-136)
17. Sermon 52 (A. II, 471)
18. Elegie XVIII, ll. 33-36 (G. 117)
19. "Sapho to Philaenis," ll. 35-38 (G. 125)
20. Elegie VIII, ll. 47-48 (G. 92)
21. Elegie III, ll. 17-18 (G. 83)

XVIII. THE HEAVENS

1. Meditation 1 (S. 2)
2. Meditation 4 (S. 16)
3. Satyre III, ll. 79-84 (G. 157)
4. "Obsequies to the Lord Harrington," l. 164 (G. 276)
5. Elegie II, l. 45 (G. 82)
6. "Ecclogue. 1613," ll. 160-162 (G. 137)
7. *Ibid.*, ll. 149-152 (G. 137)
8. *Biathanatos* (F. 153-154)
9. Verse Letter, "To the Countesse of Huntingdon," ll. 99-100 (G. 420)
10. Sermon 112 (A. IV, 564-565)
11. "Ecclogue. 1613," ll. 25-28 (G. 132)
12. Sermon 107 (A. IV, 458)
13. Ll. 143-144 (G. 235)
14. Ll. 13-14 (G. 120)
15. Verse Letter, "To the Countesse of Huntingdon," ll. 65-66 (G. 419)
16. Satyre V, ll. 90-91 (G. 171)
17. Letter to Sir H. G. (M. 54-55)
18. Verse Letter, "To Sir Henry Goodyere," ll. 9-10 (G. 183)
19. Elegie IX, "The Autumnall," ll. 1-2 (G. 92)
20. *Ibid.*, ll. 37-38 (G. 94)
21. Sermon 12 (A. I, 239)
22. "The Legacie," l. 4 (G. 20)
23. "Loves Alchymie," ll. 11-12 (G. 39)

24. "The Second Anniversary," ll. 119-120 (G. 254)
25. Sermon 91 (A. IV, 168)

XIX. RIVERS AND SEAS

1. Sermon 72 (A. III, 300-301)
2. Expostulation 19 (S. 115-116)
3. Sermon 107 (A. IV, 456)
4. Letter to his mother (H. 472)
5. "Elegie for the Lady Marckham," ll. 1-6 (G. 279)
6. *Ibid.,* l. 29 (G. 280)
7. *Ibid.,* ll. 17-20
8. Ll. 13-14 (G. 369)
9. Satyre III, ll. 103-110 (G. 158)
10. Sermon 153 (A. VI, 107-108)
11. Elegie VI, ll. 15-17 (G. 88)
12. Ll. 11-14 (G. 113)
13. Elegie III, ll. 31-35 (G. 83)
14. Ll. 21-34 (G. 88)
15. (G. 168-170)

XX. ANIMALS—REAL AND FABULOUS

1. For example, Sermon 76 (A. III, 373); Elegie XII, l. 30 (G. 101); and "La Corona," Sonnet 7, l. 10 (G. 321)
2. Sermon 38 (A. II, 169)
3. Verse Letter, "To Mr. E. G.," ll. 13-17 (G. 209) and Verse Letter, "To Mr. B. B.," ll. 2-4 (G. 212)
4. "Obsequies to the Lord Harrington," ll. 168-170 (G. 276)
5. "The Second Anniversary," ll. 55-56 (G. 253)
6. *Ibid.,* ll. 117-118 (G. 254) and Sermon 8 (A. I, 158)
7. Verse Letter, ll. 51-52 (G. 182)
8. Sermon 108 (A. IV, 487) and Sermon 35 (A. II, 122)
9. Sermon 98 (A. IV, 288)
10. Ll. 17-19 (G. 88)
11. Ll. 6-7 (G. 28)
12. Verse Letter, "To the Countesse of Bedford," ll. 83-84 (G. 198)
13. *Essays in Divinity* (J. 92-93)
14. Elegie XIII, ll. 17-18 (G. 105)
15. Sermon 156 (A. VI, 236-237)
16. (K. 68)
17. Ll. 39-42 (G. 125)
18. Ll. 56-58 (G. 182)
19. Elegie XVIII, ll. 4-6 (G. 116)
20. Elegie XVI, l. 33 (G. 112)

21. ,Sermon 13 (A. I, 254)
22. Satyre III, ll. 22-24 (G. 155)
23. "Ecclogue, 1613," ll. 171-172 (G. 138)
24. (M. 42-43)
25. (J. 92)
26. Elegie IV, ll. 7-8 (G. 84)
27. Meditation 12 (S. 67-68) and Probleme XI (K. 58)
28. Sermon 59 (A. III, 34-35)
29. Sermon 56 (A. II, 552)
30. Sermon 158 (A. VI, 283)
31. Epithalamion on the Lady Elizabeth and Count Palatine, ll. 24-27 (G. 128)
32. "The First Anniversary," ll. 216-218 (G. 238)
33. Ll. 23-27 (G. 15)
34. Sermon 29 (A. I, 579)
35. Elegie IV, ll. 47-50 (G. 85)

INDEX

268